SINGING,
ACTING,
AND
MOVEMENT
IN
Opera

MARK ROSS CLARK

LYNN V. CLARK, *Curriculum Designer*

INDIANA
University Press
Bloomington & Indianapolis

SINGING,

ACTING,

AND

MOVEMENT

IN

Opera

A Guide to Singer-getics

This book is a publication of

Indiana University Press
601 North Morton Street
Bloomington, IN 47404-3797 USA

http://iupress.indiana.edu

Telephone orders 800-842-6796
Fax orders 812-855-7931
E-mail orders iuporder@indiana.edu

The paper used in this publication meets the minimum
requirements of American National Standard for Information
Sciences—Permanence of Paper for Printed Library Materials,
ANSI Z39.48-1984.

Manufactured in the United States of America

Library of Congress Cataloging-in-Publication Data

Clark, Mark Ross, date
   Singing, acting, and movement in opera : a guide to singer-
getics / by Mark Ross Clark ; Lynn V. Clark, curriculum
designer.
      p.   cm.
Includes bibliographical references (p.   ) and index.
   ISBN 0-253-34113-2 (cloth : alk. paper) — ISBN 0-253-21532-3
(pbk. : alk. paper)
   1. Acting in opera. 2. Singing—Interpretation (Phrasing,
dynamics, etc.) I. Clark, Lynn V. II. Title.

   MT956 .C65 2002
   792.5'028—dc21
                                    2002000416

1 2 3 4 5 07 06 05 04 03 02

CONTENTS

Foreword:
A Message from Tito Capobianco

The great works of art that endure and last forever are those that never cease to produce new meanings within their interpreters, performers, readers, viewers, listeners, and audiences. To reach this state of validity in opera, an art form comprised of a "sublime ambiguity of the greatest artistic disciplines, all led by the human voice," we must provide its future artists and teachers every available tool to make possible, without limitations, new ways of expression and interpretation in our time of constant change and evolution.

The present book is a remarkable collection of observations and reflections on past experiences by many excellent artists and teachers that will doubtless help the new generation of those interested in creating "opera magic." They will find new answers to questions of emotional searching, motivation, responses to past failures, and ways of discovering, reevaluating, and affirming past values. The inclusion of many exercises encourages experimentation in finding the individuality and singularity of each artist, proving that time and again, with the discipline of the proper talent and perseverance, everything onstage can be possible.

This book clearly avoids the intellectual contradiction that denies the spontaneous and passionate "projection of emotion" that rules opera, offering innumerable avenues and a variety of ways to achieve creativity and conviction of expression.

In our contemporary state of "mega-multiculturalism," socioeconomic globalization, and technological revolution, it is extremely necessary in all of the arts, and most especially in opera, that we reconsider every aspect involved to ensure a sensitive and true participation in our own cultural future. If we want to expand the boundaries of people's perceptions, the following pages are a serious attempt to achieve just that.

Tito Capobianco
February 2001

List of Interviews

I would like to thank the following artists and experts for sharing their time and talents during interviews. Their words and wisdom have been invaluable to this book.

SINGERS

Elizabeth Futral
Franz Grundheber
Håkan Hagegård
Kevin Langan
Susanne Mentzer
Timothy Noble
Robert Orth
Jerold Siena
Frederica von Stade
Carol Vaness
Sally Wolf

CONDUCTORS

Julius Rudel
Patrick Summers

DIRECTORS

Tito Capobianco
Matthew Lata
Jay Lesenger
Joshua Major
Nicholas Muni
Harry Silverstein

COMPOSERS

Mark Adamo
William Bolcom
Jake Heggie
Kirke Mechem

COACHES

Joan Dornemann
Martin Katz
John Wustman

POSTURAL ALIGNMENT

Emily Bogard

COMBAT AND ACTING

Dale Girard

ACTING AND MOVEMENT

Robyn Hunt, University of Washington
Judy Nunn, New York City
Ann Woodsworth, Northwestern University
Evan Yionoulis, Chair, Yale School of Drama

PERFORMANCE ANXIETY

Steven Curtis, Ph.D.

ARTISTIC DIRECTORS AND MANAGERS

John Berry, English National Opera
Diana Hossack, Opera America
Gayletha Nichols, Houston Opera Studio, MET Auditions

Using the Guide

Synergism—cooperative action or operation so that the total effect is greater than the sum of the effects taken independently; derived from the Greek word *syn-ergos,* meaning to work together.

—*Webster's New International Dictionary*

This guidebook seeks to bring together the different exercises and resources that help to make an opera singer's performance synergetic—greater than the sum of its parts. A synthesis of many workshops and classes about opera skills, it can be used either by individual singers or by educators.

Traditionally, "opera workshop" has been a class that simply rehearses and performs opera scenes. It is a chance to learn repertoire and seldom allows the time or provides the tools to look deeper into the process behind the performance. Although interesting lessons in stagecraft, including period etiquette and combat, might be offered, the integration of voice, drama, and movement is often left up to the singer.

This guidebook presents a series of lessons and exercises that explore movement, dramatization, and voice and shows how these areas can be integrated. To understand the voice and how it works, singers go to a vocal teacher. To explore the methods of analyzing character and emotions, one goes to a drama coach. To understand movement and muscle function, the study of dance is useful. All three of these areas of study are important for an opera singer, but equally important is a place where the singer can make connections among the three disciplines. Singers need a safe place to juggle and experiment with the integration of voice, drama, and movement. All too often, the first time that singers are asked to present a fully integrated performance is onstage.

In my classes and workshops, I encourage singers to take chances and risk failure. I create a nonjudgmental environment that is akin to a laboratory—a place to experiment.

The emphasis is on process, not product. Each exercise is just a starting point from which singers can become "singer-getic." Much of my work has been inspired by my mentor in the area of opera training, H. Wesley Balk.

WHO CAN USE THIS GUIDEBOOK?

This guidebook is intended for those young professionals embarking upon a career as well as young singers beginning their studies. It provides curriculum for teachers of voice, opera workshop, and even choral studies. It can be used as a class textbook, a teacher's guide, or a personal handbook.

HOW CAN I USE THE GUIDEBOOK?

The guidebook is organized into three parts: "Preparation," "Integration," and "Application." Within each section are chapters that give a brief introduction to a topic followed by several exercises. A checklist at the end of the chapter provides an overview of the lesson as well as an optional writing assignment.

Depending on your goals, the materials in the guidebook can be used in order or reorganized as needed. The two-hour classes that I lead are always a "recipe" with different chapter ingredients. In one class session, singers may begin with movement exercises from Part I, Chapter 1, and listen to a lecture on period etiquette and practice bows from Part II, Chapter 7. Outside of class time, students might coach arias using exercises from Part III, Chapter 11.

As you read the guidebook, you will encounter the words of many professionals in the field of opera. Over the years I have had the privilege of interviewing some of the top performers in the world of opera. Their wisdom and insight are woven into the body of the lessons as well as highlighted in the "Meet the Artist" sections of each chapter.

WHAT SHOULD I DO FIRST ?

In the first class of the semester, I always sit down with the singers and discuss their hopes and visions. This serves to personalize the class and to open communication between the singer and instructor. I begin by asking each singer to "describe how you felt during your optimal singing performance." The idea is for singers to describe the feelings they had in association with a performance they would like to replicate. If singers start to relate a list of performance details, like a résumé, I stop and ask them to look beyond the stage, to what was happening inside.

Most often, singers will describe how they were "in the moment, not thinking what came next." They will tell how they "completely let go, yet felt in control," or how they "forgot about vocal technique . . . and felt goose bumps, joyful." As singers articulate their memories of powerful performances, they create an environment that is positive and nonjudgmental.

By using self-assessment and sharing to open the workshop sessions, you can set a tone that provides the building blocks for rapid performance growth. The environment of the workshop calls for peer feedback and self-assessment that is kept on course by the instructor. This can be done only by abolishing judgment.

WHY SHOULD I CURB CRITICAL JUDGMENT?

As a performer, we feel critical judgment coming from many directions—teachers, other singers, conductors, coaches, and ourselves. When the climate is stripped of judgment and replaced by honest, straightforward observation, the atmosphere is more conducive to playful experimentation. Such an environment can be established by the instructor from the very beginning by applauding what is positive and noting what has the potential for growth. Other singers will pick up the tone of the instructor and learn to look for the positive aspects of performance in others and, most importantly, themselves.

This guidebook is filled with exercises that allow an individual or class to create powerful performances through isolating and then integrating the body, facial expression, and application of character and setting. However, these are only the tools of the performer.

There is no one formula to reach a powerful performance. The numerous interviews with artists and experts reveal that there is not one path. Each singer-actor possesses an individuality from which he or she draws his or her power. This comes from discipline, intense preparation through analysis and exercise, and an ability to "let go." Most importantly, they learn to trust their instincts, or intuition. It is a base from which every singer can take flight.

As you work through this guidebook, be aware of the many options from which you can choose. This choice is often spontaneous rather than practiced and polished. That is not to say we do not prepare ourselves and hone our tools. By being both prepared and yet open to those moments of mystery, we can truly be greater than the sum of our parts. We can be "singer-getic."

SINGING,
ACTING,
AND
MOVEMENT
IN
Opera

Part I. Preparation

Before walking onstage, one must prepare offstage. A powerful perfor-mance begins with an awareness of the body. It is built on efficient pos-ture and shows in the expressive face of the performer. It is supported by research into a character and framed by a rich environment. In essence, these tools provide a base upon which the performer can firmly stand— prepared and ready to sing.

Body Awareness
Stretching for Flexibility and Power

INTRODUCTION

First we move. Before we sing, we must be aware of our body. We take a deep breath, and the heart pumps faster, the blood flows to the extremities, the muscles flex and stretch, and we take a step forward. It is important to begin the exploration of movement with stretching exercises. They provide body awareness and the focus of balance, flexibility, grace, and breathing that is regular even in the face of intense emotion.

When we stretch together at the beginning of class, we are beginning to work together. As we stretch, breathe, and become more aware of our bodies, we are also interacting as we breathe and move together.

I highly recommend ballet, aerobics, and strength training for general health and a feeling of well-being. Ballet develops grace, and aerobics and strength training develop muscular tone. I like to apply yoga, t'ai chi, and Suzuki exercises to my work in opera workshop because not only do they highlight the same skills needed onstage (breathing, balance, and focus), but they are movements that are introspective as well. For example, the ability to be self-aware and at the same time focus our energy outside the body is something one needs in both yoga and singing.

Why is it important to begin with movement?

I always warm up my voice before I sing. In the same way, I become aware of my body, my breathing, and the muscles of the face before I integrate my singing with movement. Movement not only unlocks the power of the body; it releases the tension that is sometimes brought on by singing. It jump-starts the breathing and gets the blood flowing to muscles that help us to sing and move onstage.

How does yoga prepare me for singing?

Yoga is centered on breathing and positions that are similar to sustained gestures onstage. In opera the time frame is slowed, but the muscles and gestures should not be "locked" or "held." The same is true in the practice of yoga. A sustained yoga position must still have breathing, energy, and letting go of the muscles, to continue a position without discomfort.

What is the purpose of t'ai chi exercises?

T'ai chi is continuous, purposeful movement, always sustained by the breath. It is strong, and it is focused with a directed energy. In t'ai chi, the "chi," or center, is located right above the diaphragm. It is the engine that drives every movement. Because singers also focus on their diaphragm for breath support, t'ai chi can help them to visualize this "center" and maximize its power. Singers learn not only to sing "on the breath" but also to move "on the breath" with muscles that are fully oxygenated and energized.

What are some other ways to practice movement?

Stretching exercises, such as those done before athletic exercise, prepare our bodies for graceful and coordinated movement. They bring breath and energy into all of our tasks and circulate more blood to the brain. But stretching is not always enough. Sometimes we must flex to concentrate our energy while keeping our body free from tension.

In singing, strength is very important. Most singers recognize the importance of the diaphragm and the muscles of the abdomen in singing. However, muscles that are contracted can produce tension through "shortening" the spine and tightening all of the muscles. It is very common to see the singer as he or she begins a difficult passage move his or her hands upward as the arms tighten and the abdomen contracts. By taking control of our body and increasing our ability to flex and stretch, we can make the muscles lengthen rather than contract during singing. We will have just as much strength, but with more balance, flexibility, movement of breath, and less tension.

Although there are many different systems of movement in the theatrical and operatic world, one intriguing method was originated by Tadashi Suzuki, one of the foremost figures in Japanese contemporary theater. His training method is drawn from Japanese theater tradition and discipline from the 1400s and the Nô Theater. Suzuki training emphasizes the language of the

Meet the Artist: ROBYN HUNT

Robyn Hunt received her training at University of California, San Diego. A member of Actor's Equity, Professor Hunt has acted professionally in the United States, Canada, Europe, and Japan. She has worked for a decade with Tadashi Suzuki and since 1994 has performed frequently at the Actor's Theatre of Louisville, under the direction of Jon Jory. Ms. Hunt was cofounder and first artistic director of the San Diego Public Theatre. She coheads the Pacific Performance Project. Currently she teaches the Suzuki Method and acting courses in the Professional Actor Training Program at the University of Washington in Seattle.

When I interviewed Ms. Hunt, she took care to point out the difference between exercises and training. "Mr. Suzuki rarely called what we did on the stage 'exercises,'" she said, "seeking instead to get us to think about each moment of training as being equal in intensity, precision, and concentration to the moments of performance." She

went on to describe how this internal shift helped to "activate the actor's 'inner sensibility,' bringing his physical articulateness, strength, expressiveness, and power up to the same potency as his analytical mind."[2]

Ms. Hunt begins her classes with a warm-up. Actors take time to stretch, do vocal warm-ups, and walk through their staging rapidly without speaking. The warm-up is followed by training. For example, students may practice "kicking and sliding" (see Exercise 1.8). Standing in a "ready" position, they kick out the right leg with the thigh parallel to the floor and the knee bent. Next, they bring the foot to the floor with a very strong, quick motion, but do not strike the floor. Instead, they feel an upward energy as the foot descends. The foot then slides along the floor and provides the base for the movement to be repeated on the other side. Ms Hunt believes this sort of training increases "concentration, power in speaking, clarity of physical expression, and the capacity for transformation."[3]

---

feet, the strength of core support (thighs), and the "stillness" of the arms, hands, shoulders, and face.[1] (See Meet the Artist: Robyn Hunt.)

Why is it important to learn to relax?

Relaxation does not mean that the muscles are limp. It means that the body is functioning without tension and with energy. No matter what you are doing, it is important to be free of tension physically, emotionally, and mentally. When starting to work with opera singers, the great acting teacher Stanislavsky always began with relaxation exercises.[4]

1. Tadashi Suzuki, *The Way of Acting*, trans. J. Thomas Rimer (New York: Theatre Communications Group, 1986).
2. Robyn Hunt, Interview by author, e-mail, 27 November 2000.
3. Ibid.
4. Experience Brian, "Stanislavsky and the Classical Singer," *Classical Singer*, October 2000.

Many singers suffer from extraneous physical movements, muscular and facial tensions, and posture problems. Without the preparatory relaxation, all the tension and bad habits magnify and compound within the heightened state of performance. Stanislavsky said that relaxation exercises were unnecessary for "singing mannequins" but were essential "for living human beings." He warned that if performers "wish to remain alive on the stage, they are imperative."[5]

Exercises

1.1 WARM-UP

Objective: Releasing tension, feeling the weight of the arms from the shoulders so that the hands/arms/shoulders do not rise during singing.

Directions: Start by shrugging shoulders, loosening them up, and shaking out the arms. Add loose twists, swinging the arms. Bend at the hips, and touching the floor, allow the weight of the head and arms to hang until all of the tension is released. Then slowly "roll up" vertebra by vertebra to a vertical position.

1.2 PENDULUM SWING

Objective: Releasing the tension of the shoulder/neck area, awareness of the weight of the arms that will affect the gesture.

Directions: Let the weight of your upper body fall to the floor, bending at the hips, swing sweeping the floor, then swing into a sustained position, back and arms parallel to the floor. Lift your shoulders as high as possible, then let go. Feel the weight of the arms.

1.3 STRETCHING

Objective: Developing focus while engaged in a physical task.

Directions: From lying down on the back position, lift the head and find a point on which to fix your focus. It can be an object on the wall or ceiling, or something imaginary. Begin as slowly as possible to move upward, continuing to breathe and to keep the focus fixed. This movement can be practiced to a standing position. It is a very important exercise to find focus and sustain energy simultaneously.

1.4 YOGA WARM-UP

Objective: Breathing, focus/concentration, coordination, release of tension.

5. Ibid., p. 5.

Directions:
- Cobra—lie on stomach, stretch up to the ceiling with head and feet to-gether (strengthens back, nervous system, eyes).
- Tree pose—Standing on one leg, arms up and hands together (helps concentration, opens the hips).
- Bolt pose—like diving into the water (lifts diaphragm, tones back and stomach).
- Mountain pose—exercise for energetic standing.
- Virasana—sitting on legs (stretches knees).
- Child's pose—on knees, head to floor (stimulates respiration, com-presses diaphragm).

1.5 PARTNER STRETCHES

Objective: Working together.

Directions: One partner sits on the floor, the other leans over and pulls their arms, which lengthens spine and brings tailbone up and out.
- One partner in a childlike pose, the other partner presses on either side of spine. Don't press on the spine itself.
- Arm pulls: Lying down, one partner is pulling the other's arms up and out. Repeat with leg pulls the same way.
- Neck stretch: Take your partner's head in your hands and gently move from side to side. Your partner should release their neck and let you take control of the movement.

1.6 T'AI CHI

Objective: Controlling movement without tension; grace and flexibility.

Directions: Begin with hands together (all in a continuous, slow-moving fluid flow).

Breathe in as your hands rise above head, focus straight ahead, then let your arms fall in an arc down to the side. Reach up, then intertwine your hands up again. Breathe in as you begin a lunge to the right, one arm out and pushing into the lunge area as the other arm is behind the back. Then breathe out as the lunge is released into the other direction. Breathe in, moving in the op-posite direction in a lunge.

1.7 THE UNIVERSAL POST

Objective: Maintaining energy without tension.

Directions: Assume an upright position with the weight on the right foot; the other foot is extended in front, lightly touching the ground. The knees should be relaxed and arms extended in front with relaxed elbows as if grasping a fence post.

1.8 SUZUKI

Objective: Unleashing energy "into the floor" while the face, neck, shoulders, and arms remain impassive—without tension. The footwork is of utmost importance.

Directions:

- Kicking and sliding

    1. Stand in a "ready" position with your arms relaxed and balanced, low breath. Kick the right leg out and sustain the thigh parallel to the floor—with the knee bent.

    2. Move, with a very strong, quick motion, the foot to the floor, being careful not to strike the foot on the floor, but instead feel an upward energy at the same time to prevent slamming the foot to the floor.

    3. Slide the foot-body forward on the floor, keeping the left foot stationary.

    4. Kick the left foot, continuing the motion as you did with the right.

- Statues seated with focus shifts

    1. Keep contact with the hips on the floor.

    2. Sustain the "statue" with the feet both off the ground.

    3. Change the statue and eye focus with each clapped signal.

- Statues standing

    1. Keep legs and feet stationary on floor.

    2. Sustain the statue, keep breathing, free the body from tension.

    3. Change the statue and eye focus with each clapped signal.

- Relationship statues

    1. The class is divided into small groups. One group at a time is out front.

    2. On the clapped signal, standing or seated statues makes a interactive "picture" in a clear relationship within the group. This "snapshot" describes the relationship through body and facial expression.

1.9 CROSS-COUNTRY SKIING

Objective: Warming up, balance, energized movement without tension.

Directions: One leg is stationary, the other moves in a rhythmic forward and backward stepping motion while the arms move in opposition, simulating the action of a cross-country skier.

Sun Salutation (*Surya-namaskar*) instruction

The Sanskrit word *tri* means three and **kona** means corner or angle. Thus "three corner or three angle posture" is often called the triangle posture.

①  Stand facing the direction of the sun with both feet touching. Bring the hands together, palm-to-palm, at the heart.	② Inhale and raise the arms upward. Slowly bend backward, stretching arms above the head.	③ Exhale slowly bending forward, touching the earth with respect until hands are in line with the feet, head touching knees.
④ Inhale and move the right leg back away from the body in a wide backward step. Keep the hands and feet firmly on the ground, with the left foot between the hands. Raise the head.	⑤ While exhaling, bring the left foot together with the right. Keep arms straight, raise the hips and align the head with the arms, forming an upward arch.	⑥ Inhale and slowly lower the hips to the floor, (hips should be slightly raised above the ground) and bend backwards as much as possible.
⑦  Exhale and lower the body to the floor until the feet, knees, hands, chest, and forehead are touching the ground.	⑧  Inhale and slowly raise the head and bend backwards as much as possible, bending the spine to the maximum.	⑨ While exhaling slowly and keeping the arms straight, raise the hips and align the head with the arms, forming an upward arch.
⑩ Slowly inhale and bend the left leg at the knee taking a wide forward step. Keeping the hands firmly rooted, place the left foot on the ground between the hands. Lift the head upwards.	⑪ Exhale slowly and keeping hands firmly in place, bring both feet together to align them with the hands. Touch the head to the knees, if possible.	⑫ Inhale slowly and raise the arms upward. Slowly bend backwards, stretching the arms above the head. Return to position #1.

Graphics courtesy of Yoga Anand Ashram.

1.10 SALUTE TO THE SUN

Objective: Coordinating yoga positions.

Directions: The Salute to the Sun is an excellent exercise after the stretching exercises that isolate the parts of the body. The Salute to the Sun is a series of poses that midway through retrograde back to the beginning. Each pose at first will be separately learned and practiced and soon will "flow" from one pose to another with grace, strength, and purpose. Breathing and momentum are important; lack of tension and flow of energy are crucial.

CONCLUSION

Exercises in yoga, t'ai chi, and Suzuki training focus on those movements of the body that are especially useful to the singer-actor onstage. Singing actors need to be aware of their body, their sense of balance, and their breath. While a powerful energy is needed to produce a voice that can sing over an orchestra, tension that accompanies this energy is counterproductive. Movement exercises release this tension and help singers find a "peaceful center." In addition, singers become physically stronger and benefit from the energy of breathing and moving together.

CHECKLIST

- Take a deep, low breath.
- Drop shoulders to feel weight of the arms.
- Have a balance that originates from a strong center.
- Maintain energy without tension.
- Make a list of four exercises you can do every day before singing. Explain why you chose those particular exercises.

Postural
Aligning the Body

2

INTRODUCTION

The importance of alignment while singing is well documented. Poor posture affects the flow of breath, and faulty alignment can create tension that affects the throat and the act of singing. During performance, movement that is powerful but free from tension is essential to the act of singing. This extends to standing, sitting, and whatever position the director may ask you to assume while singing.

There is a common misconception that when a singer stands onstage, he or she should "hold" the shoulders and chest high in an unnatural performing stance. This posture produces an unnatural performance. When someone stands, walks, and sits one way in daily life and another way onstage, it rings false to those in the audience and to the performer. By practicing efficient posture in your daily life, you can extend that alignment to the stage.

Isn't good posture just standing up straight?

On the contrary, "good" posture is when the body is aware of the natural curvature of the spine. When our parents told us to "stand up straight," the shoulders were pulled back, and this created tension in the back, shoulders, and neck.

What does it feel like to be in alignment?

Strong, purposeful, and efficient posture feels free, and the spine feels long, extending into the skull. The skull alone weighs around twelve pounds, or nearly that of a bowling ball. It perches at the top of the spine. We also feel the weight of the bones of the arms, allowing the shoulders to be calm and not lifted. Balance is important, which means our spine may not feel straight when it is aligned. We will feel energy through the body even while we are standing still, for we are still breathing and feeling the extension of the spine.

How can I align the different parts of my body?

For the performing artist, alignment refers to the ordering of weight through the skeletal framework to provide stability and responsiveness when executing a movement. One can align the body by finding a center of balance, extending the spine without tension, and keeping the knees flexible. Instead of tucking the posterior in, the natural curve of the spine may bring your hips out a little. This is more natural than pulling your hips forward, which then forces you to lock your knees and lose balance. When the spine is lengthened, the weight of the head on the spine is lessened, helping the body with balance and strength.

Alignment is not solely for an aesthetic look of strength for the singing actor; it is imperative for free vocal production and freedom of movement. Acting teacher Robyn Hunt suggests opening a channel between the feet, the legs, the pelvis, and the voice. "We seek in the work to have the actor speaking the character's 'truth,' a truth that is not overly protested from the neck up, with the head overly gesticulating and punching words, but rather a sound and set of ideas that seem to come up—as the truth does—from the feet, the floor, the pelvis, the center."[1]

Where is my center?

Each singer needs to find that place, whether standing or sitting, that is a balanced position from which all movement takes place. It is an aesthetically pleasing pose that also looks natural. When we are fully in balance, we have found a sustained place of readiness. We have the possibility of moving in any direction without losing our balance, and we are prepared to move or sustain our pose.

How can I feel energy and strength when my voice teacher keeps telling me to stand still?

For the singer to be able to have a feeling of strength, flowing energy, and flexibility, he or she must stand without "holding" the body. Examine the changes that we go through physically when we sing up into the highest range, or through a cadenza of great difficulty. The spine and the arms want

---

1. Robyn Hunt, Interview by author, e-mail, 27 November 2000.

to shorten and pull toward the body. This is when we feel the entire body pull into the center with the vocal support mechanism. The hands want to gesture together with the arms pulling up in a "half gesture" of little meaning.

By letting go of tension, you can bring your body back into alignment. Try releasing the skeletal weight of the arms and allowing the arms to hang, freeing the shoulders and neck from tension. Allow the spine to lengthen, and see how the strength of support comes from elongation rather than contraction. This may take some getting used to, because when we go through our most intricate vocal passages and into our highest range, that is not the time we in-

---

Meet the Artist: EMILY BOGARD

Emily Bogard is a former dancer and choreographer. Her background in modern dance and ballet eventually led to an interest in the structure and function of the human body. She studied how the poise of the skeletal system affects alignment and movement. Drawing from her studies of Pilates (a method of physical and mental conditioning developed by Joseph Pilates, 1880–1967), the Alexander Technique, and the body-mind principles of Bonnie Bainbridge-Cohen, Ms. Bogard teaches an approach to alignment that enables performing artists, visual artists, and people from all walks of life to enjoy a physical freedom based on spinal stability and mobility.

In her classes Ms. Bogard counsels that "our basic postural organization supports our self-use in day-to-day activities as well as our artistic performance. This organization is the foundation from which a singer builds a character or presents him- or herself in an audition, competition, or recital. Being able to observe oneself and become aware of self-use in daily patterns of movement tasks such as opening a door, brushing your teeth, or sitting at a computer will lead to a better understanding and keener perception of postural alignment during vocal production."[2] In short, efficient use of the body prevents overexertion, strain, and fatigue. (See Appendix B for Ms. Bogard's "Postural Alignment.")

---

stinctively feel we should let go, stretch, and free ourselves. However, once you set this pattern, you will eventually feel less vulnerable and more powerful, even while standing "still."

How important is good posture in real life?

It is not enough to have good posture onstage or in the studio. How you move onstage should be the same as how you move in the "real world." Not only can healthy singers not afford the injuries and fatigue brought on by poor

---

2. Emily Bogard, Workshop in residence, Indiana University, June 1999.

posture, but their posture will not "ring true" if they stand one way onstage and another way at home.

The next time you are sitting in a chair, check to see that you are in balance. Can you breathe easily? While you are walking or jogging, feel the weight of your arms, and keep your shoulders low, while lengthening the spine. When you get in a car, release the neck and shoulder muscles before checking for blind spots. Finally, always lift with the legs, using the hips and not the back for support. Set these good habits in life, and they will come naturally onstage. Veteran stage director Tito Capobianco always begins a class with the question, "What is your instrument?"[3] The answer: Your whole body.

Exercises

2.1 STANDING

Objective: Finding the most efficient way of standing without tension.

Directions: The feet should be apart on the floor equal to the width of your shoulders. Round the shoulders forward radically to the point of hunching. This creates tension, and the knees will be pulled back and possibly locked. Then go in the opposite direction, in which the shoulders are pulled back, also with tension. The hips are pushed forward.

Although this position feels stiff and unnatural, it is not unlike a posture that is affected onstage. In the process of going back and forth slowly between the rounded and pulled back shoulders and the hips and knees following, find the exact center of balance in which there is an absence of tension.

2.2 SITTING

Objective: Finding the balance in sitting.

Directions: This exercise can be done on the floor or on a chair with your feet on the floor. Let the shoulders fall and slump forward. Very slowly and gradually, bring the shoulders, back, and head back as you begin to arch backwards. At a specific point in this process, you will feel a click as the hip girdle pulls back on the "sitting bone" beneath you. As you go between the two positions and are just "up on the sitting bone," you will find that balanced place from which you can sing and stand if you wish without tension.

2.3 SITTING TO STANDING

Objective: Moving from sitting to standing in a flowing manner with momentum and without tension.

3. Tito Capobianco, Workshop in residence, Indiana University, February 2001.

Directions: Find your balanced sitting position with your feet firmly on the floor. When ready to stand, bring the head forward first in a continuous motion, and with momentum go forward, using the legs for support. Avoid the crutch of involving the shoulders or back, which will halt this momentum.

2.4 LONG NECK AND JAW

Objective: Feeling the lengthening of the neck with a free jaw.

Directions: Clasp your hands, then place them on the back of your neck. Pull apart the fingers in the direction of your back and head to feel the length of the neck. Pull both hands across from your ears down your jaw to your mouth, feeling a full release of the jaw.

2.5 WALKING

Objective: Freeing the arms, walking naturally.

Directions: When walking onstage, you will notice that some actors "hold" their arms without allowing them to swing naturally, and this rings false. Allow the skeletal weight of the arms to be free from the shoulders and swing in a natural range of motion. Feel strength in the core support of the thighs and hips, and feel that your body is directed toward a goal. Feel flexibility in the ankles and feel the feet push into the floor with strength. The knees should be free and released.

CONCLUSION

The way we sing, how we stand, and how comfortably we sit in a chair is shaped by our posture. When our posture is aligned, it helps us to accomplish all these tasks with movement that is purposeful and free from tension. The positions of flow of yoga described in Chapter 1 are also helpful for sustaining a posture while learning to let go and breathe. In addition, I recommend the Alexander Technique as described by Emily Stuart (see Appendix B), and the Feldenkrais Method (for more information visit http://www.feldenkrais.com).

"Good" posture is never held or frozen, but is filled with energy and in constant motion. Singers often sustain a gesture or a position while singing, but this does not mean that the energy stops or that we lose our flexibility of motion. Done correctly, posture can be the power behind a powerful performance.

CHECKLIST

- Stand with a feeling of the spine stretched into the skull and the knees flexible. Feel the weight of the arms, which allows the shoulders to rest without tension. Allow the natural curve of the spine.

- Sustain, but do not hold, this posture.
- Walk with the head high without tension, and a natural swing to the arms. Lead with the heart (not hips or head). Keep the knees and ankles flexible.
- Walk purposefully with direction and strength.
- Sit with both feet on the floor, spine stretched into the skull, hips balanced forward, with arms heavy.
- Keep breathing for energy and power.
- Describe in writing how you feel when you are in alignment—standing, walking, sitting. Compare it to the way you normally feel during those same activities.

The Expressive Face
Communicating Emotions Onstage

3

INTRODUCTION

The eyes and face are powerful channels for energy and indicators of a specific emotion. The more specific the expression, the more the audience will receive a clear message. This is the key to communication: clarity. The expressive face is a face that is alive with thought. It reflects the singer's imagination "in the moment" and invites the audience to share that moment.

Many singers believe they must feel the emotion they want to express. This type of "method" acting can produce powerful performances, but it also can lead to vocal and physical tension. If the singer's face is not expressive, the performer may feel the emotion more than the audience does. An emotional performance is often the product of an expressive face.

An expressive face can serve as a catalyst for not only the audience feeling an emotion, but the singer as well. By wearing an expression of anger without actually being angry, the singer can feel the stirrings of that emotion without the physical tension. The expression is controlled—a mask that can be put on and taken off at will—and does not interfere with vocal technique.

What makes a face expressive?

Focus suggests a moving energy, like a ball in a constant state of movement, the players all acutely conscious of everything going on around them while keeping their eye on the ball.

—*Viola Spolin,* Improvisation for the Theater[1]

1. Viola Spolin, *Improvisation for the Theater*, 3d ed. (Evanston, Ill.: Northwestern University Press, 1999), 2d ed. preface.

Important elements of the expressive face are the eyes and their focus. To take the model from real life, expressive eyes are eyes that focus both outwardly and inwardly. A singer's eyes can focus on another singer onstage or reminisce by reliving the experience via "seeing" what the text describes. For example, in Mozart's *Le Nozze di Figaro*, Susanna sings the recitative to the aria "Deh vieni non tardar":

> Giunse alfin il momento che godrò senz' affanno / in braccio all' idol mio.
>
> (At last arrives the moment, which will come without worry / in the arms of him who I worship.)[2]

Looking at the line that proceeds this recitative, Susanna speaks an aside to herself *sotto voce* that reveals that she knows Figaro is hiding ("Il birbo è in sentinella"). This moment gives her the opportunity to focus toward a make-believe lover, driving Figaro even further into a jealous rage that was exacerbated during his preceding aria "Aprite un po' quegl' occhi." During this make-believe address to a "lover," the musical interludes give Susanna an opportunity to focus back to Figaro only with her eyes, curious to know his reaction, while still enjoying the joke on him.

There is also an opportunity for a change in focus from the imagined lover to Figaro hiding in the bushes when Susanna begins to describe what she sees in nature. At this point, it is crucial for Susanna to specifically "see" and not generalize. This moment has the potential of changing her mood from a superficial playfulness to a deep appreciation of the beauty of her surroundings. As she sings, she is very descriptive:

> Quì mormora il ruscel, quì scherza l'aura, che col dolce susurro il cor ristaura, quì ridono i fioretti, e l'erba è fresca, ai piaceri d'amor qui tutto adesca.
>
> (The stream murmurs, the playful breeze, which with sweetness whispers to a refreshed heart, flowers, and fresh grass, the pleasures that entice love.)[3]

When Susanna looks and "sees" these specific references to her surroundings, they stimulate her memory. Could she have spent time in this garden with Figaro? This is an opportunity for Susannah to shift from the "game" to reveal her true feelings about Figaro. This scene is but one example of the importance of focus. Eyes that are alive with thought and truly "see" rather than are fixed in an unfocused stare are compelling to an audience.

2. Translated by Edoardo Lèbano.
3. Ibid.

Meet the Artist: **ELIZABETH FUTRAL**

American soprano Elizabeth Futral has been called one of her generation's leading lyric-coloratura sopranos for her rich, vibrant voice and captivating stage personality. She is known for her powerful performances and intense focus. When I asked how she maintains this focus, she replied, "When I am completely immersed in a role, I do what seems natural with my eyes. That sounds too simple, but it is true in that I don't isolate my focus from the rest of my character's actions."[4] Her simple and direct focus comes from reactions to what is said and done onstage, from inner thoughts, and from memories.

I recently spoke with stage director and teacher Jay Lesenger, the Artistic Director of the Chautauqua Opera. He had just finished directing Ms. Futral in a production of Donizetti's *Lucia di Lammermoor.* Before working with Mr. Lesenger, Ms. Futral had sung the title role for her debut at the Metropolitan Opera. Mr. Lesenger found her portrayal to be "Very interesting, possessing a vulnerability with strength."[5] However, he wanted to do something different with the mad scene (act 3, scene 2).

The mad scene in *Lucia* is a classic opportunity for a singing actor to engage the audience with a powerful performance. This is accomplished not only with the voice, but also with the power of the face and focus of the eyes. Traditionally, Lucia's focus is pulled into herself— she is isolated in her madness. But Lesenger wanted the audience to see what Lucia "sees." So the ghosts Lucia sings of manifest themselves at the ruined well and later reappear in her famous mad scene. She mistakes guests at the party for her spurned lover and her murdered husband. Ms. Futral is a terrific singing actress. She seized upon this opportunity with relish. As the scene progressed, Lucia/Futral shifted her focus from these external apparitions to deep within herself and back. So Lucia's madness became much more specific. In her hands, this clarity of focus allowed the audience to enter into her madness.[6]

What should I do about the rest of the face?

The muscles of the face are extremely important tools for the singer and are underused by most of us. It remains a difficult task for singers to simultaneously open the vowels, loosen and drop the jaw, and use the muscles of the face in an expressive, concentrated energy without bringing tension into vocal production.

The best way to bring the face into full use is through using two different approaches. First, flex the facial muscles, sustain the mask, and then integrate that flex with the singing voice (see Exercise 3.1). Next, try to sustain an expression while singing. The leader can do this by holding up an imaginary camera and pretending to take a "snapshot" of a sustained expression. Once

4. Elizabeth Futral, Interview by author, telephone, 22 September 2000.
5. Jay Lesinger, Interview by author, telephone, February 2001.
6. Ibid.

the expression is sustained, the singer can check his or her jaw tension and position to see if the throat can be free of tension while the muscles of the face sustain energy. Once the singer sees that this is possible, the game can go on, and he or she can work with increased intensity of expression while singing scales or a set piece of music.

How do I know what my face is doing?

In class I use a simple hand signal to request increased facial expression — a circular motion in front of the singer's face. When tension comes into the face or body, a simple motion of the right arm and hand signifying a little toss of tension over the right shoulder asks the singer to release tension, to let go. When the singer accomplishes any of these tasks, I, and other singers in the class, outline a large "Y" with the hands and arms to communicate an emphatic YES to the singer. Wesley Balk, author of *The Complete Singer-Actor* and *Performing Power,* first introduced me to this system of hand signals.[7] I have used the system for many years in opera workshops and private coaching. Although there are many benefits to this system, two points are crucial: (1) the signals, when two students work together using them—one singing and one leading—promote interaction without judgment, and (2) the visual stimulus allows the singer to continue singing without stopping.

How can I communicate different emotions?

Another exercise utilized by Wesley Balk in his workshops stimulates the inner emotion, which results in the emotional expression. He uses "attitude cards" which can be employed in a number of ways. These cards can be rapidly displayed for the singers to communicate the emotions without rehearsal. During the exercise, the singer realizes that he or she can find a specific emotion quickly without thinking about it and figuring out how to locate it.[8] Instead, these emotions can be sustained and magnified with the voice (see Exercise 3.6).

Another important value of the attitude cards is to bring specificity into the singer's expression. Singers will tend to generalize emotions. They should realize that there is an enormous spectrum of emotions available to us (see Appendix A). These emotions, or attitudes, can be made clear to the audience through exercise and feedback. Clear communication of specific emotions

7. H. Wesley Balk, *The Complete Singer-Actor* (Minneapolis: University of Minnesota Press, 1985).
    8. Ibid.

offers clarity over generalization. It offers specificity of choice over no choice at all.

Must I feel an emotion inside to communicate it onstage?

To create, say, anger in a character, a student would be instructed only to add the quality of anger to his face rather than search for a past or internal motivation.
—*Michael Chekhov,* On the Technique of Acting[9]

Michael Chekhov performed in Stanislavsky's company but broke with him philosophically because he believed that the stimulus for an actor's source of inspiration, feeling, and expressiveness should always begin outside the private and internalized world of the performer. The substitution for the Stanislavsky sense of memory and emotional recall comes from the external expression of adding an emotional "quality," or attitude.

This path to emotional expression is especially helpful to the singer, who with an internal stimulus of anger will often experience problems in sustaining this emotion while trying to effect the proper muscle coordination for singing. Evidence for this is commonplace on the dramatic stage. An actor who is portraying rage will often experience his or her voice tightening down and rising in pitch. This renders the dramatic value of the voice as impotent instead of utilizing it as an important "power tool." However, this approach does not exclude finding the emotion through association with one's self. Emotional memory can be vitally important as long as there is a release of tension when emotion builds.

Exercises

3.1 FACE FLEX

Objective: Isolating muscles in the face.

Directions: Sit and flex the muscles symmetrically (left and right together) and then asymmetrically. Flex the muscles at the forehead, around the nose, and around the mouth. Add simple vocal production to it, starting with a hum and then opening into a vowel while continuing to flex the facial muscles.

Extend the exercise by trying to sing with a sustained expression — or snapshot of the attitude. When the expression is sustained in a "mask," you can feel the expression in the forehead, eyes, and cheeks, while the jaw and throat are free and released.

9. Michael Chekhov, *On the Technique of Acting,* ed. Mel Gordon (New York: Harper-Collins, 1991), p. xxviii.

3.2 FOCUS

Objective: Looking and seeing.

Directions: Find an object in the room and examine it. Do not merely look at it, examine the object intensely. Note what your eyes and face are doing. Now focus on a memory. Note the change in your eye position.

3.3 EXAMINE THE PROP

Objective: Maintaining full focus and curious examination of the prop.

Directions: An object will be given to you. Examine the prop. Turn it in the light. Note what your eyes and face are doing. Share your examination of the prop and your reactions with the audience.

3.4 OBSERVATION OF CHILD

Objective: Viewing how "pure" emotions and intense focus can be as observed in children.

Directions: Observe a young child watching television. Far from the "hypnotized" look we think we will see, there is much to be learned when we watch these children. The child takes in everything and reflects emotions without filters of any kind. The child does not have the emotional inhibitions of guarding or hiding the emotions, and there is nothing "false" about the expression.

3.5 FOCUS SHIFT

Objective: Clarifying focus shifts.

Directions: In its simplest state, a focus shift will represent the face/eyes thinking about one subject in focus. The next thought will be signified by the eyes shifting with the thought process followed by the face.

These focus shifts are not restricted to the singing phrases. They are also an important part of the singing actor's expression during instrumental introductions, interludes, and especially the concluding phrases of the orchestra after the singer's final notes.

3.6 ATTITUDES

Objective: Communicating an emotion that is clear to the audience.

Directions: Attitude cards can easily be made up from the list in Appendix A (place one word per card). They can be used in many different ways. One of the best ways to introduce them is to hold them up one at a time in rapid succession without an opportunity for the student to "rehearse" the emotion or try to associate it with personal experience.

It is a powerful realization indeed to rapidly "find" these emotions without time to prepare. After this rapid practice, integrate the attitudes with the sustained masks, and later introduce vocalization through the addition of scales. Coordinate the focus shift with the attitude shift.

3.7 FOCUS WHILE THE BODY IS WORKING

Objective: Maintaining an observant focus while the body is working.

Directions: Lie down on the floor, bring the head off the floor. Focus on an object you can see and examine. Slowly bring the body up to seated position while focusing on and examining an object.

Variation: Sing a tone to check there is airflow and no glottal "holds."

CONCLUSION

Exercising the face and expressions and shifting focus are as important as exercising the voice and body. Think about the energy that comes from the eyes, the face, and a strong emotion. A powerful performance channels that energy and invites the audience to enter the emotional life of a character.

The expressive face is one way a performer can communicate his or her emotions. A clear focus, a specific expression, and a distinct shift to the next emotion guide the audience along the same path as the performer's. The emotional journey is no longer solitary; it is shared.

CHECKLIST

- Recognize the concentrated energy that comes through a clear focus and specific expression.
- Communicate a specific emotion/attitude using your face and focus shifts.
    1. Focus on a specific location.
    2. Add a specific expression (emotion) or "attitude."
    3. Shift focus to a new location.
    4. Change expression.
- Write down how you feel inside as you practice different focus shifts.
- Examine how it feels to delineate the focus by different thoughts going to separate focus areas, much like we do in everyday conversation.

Character Study
Decoding the Clues to Character

INTRODUCTION

Character study is an integral part of the preparation of a complete singer-actor. The in-depth exploration of a character prepares the singer to make decisions that present a clear emotional picture, and a performance that is in focus and not generalized. It has the potential of unlocking a singer's imagination and providing the core of a powerful and meaningful performance. Stage director Tito Capobianco talks about the "conviction" of the singer that comes from motivation and intent. It is this conviction that supports the vitality of the character.[1]

If we study a character and the person becomes real to us, then that character can come alive onstage. But to study a character we need to blur the lines between music, text, and movement. We must look at all the facets of opera and, at the same time, remain open to our own feelings. Yes, the director will guide us, stimulate us, and help us make decisions as the scene unfolds, but it is a deep understanding of the character that breathes life into a role.

What is the first step in creating a character study?

An artist's creative imagination immediately goes into high gear when he or she describes the play and the character without having a chance to think and analyze it, before forming intellectual preconceptions.

—*Michael Chekhov,* On the Technique of Acting[2]

The first step to a successful character study often precedes learning the

1. Tito Capobianco, Interview by author, Indiana University residency, February 2001.
2. Michael Chekhov, *On the Technique of Acting,* ed. Mel Gordon (New York: Harper-Collins, 1991), p. 160.

text and music. Michael Chekhov suggests that, upon examining the libretto for the first time, the performer be aware of his or her own reaction to the character. Chekhov counsels actors to paraphrase the story and find what resonates with their own feelings: "Listen to the words, to the voices, see the feelings of the characters and inwardly follow their desires."[3]

I believe that the best way to begin an opera character study is to approach the character as a detective might, looking for clues to their identity. First, translate and read the libretto thoroughly. Underline words and phrases that you find meaningful. Next, look at the cast list in the front of the score for the designation of the character, their title, or their relationship to other characters. Then look through the libretto for textual clues that help give you insights about the character.

A well-constructed opera should highlight important attributes of a character when he or she is first introduced. When the curtain opens on Puccini's *La Bohème*, two young men, a painter and a poet, are very cold and hungry, but they are also laughing about their circumstances. At the beginning of Verdi's *La Traviata*, after a brief prelude that presents musical themes from the opera, the curtain opens to reveal a party scene with Violetta as the life of the party. The opening scene of Carlisle Floyd's *Susannah* shows a square dance interrupted by Olin Blitch's introduction as well as the entrance of Susannah. In this first glimpse of Susannah, we see the contrast between her youthful spirit and the rigidity of the elders' wives. Each opening scene provides important clues to the main characters.

Where are the musical clues?

Most of the definition of character is through the music. . . . A great deal is dictated by the music and the composer's view of the character.

—*Frederica von Stade*[4]

To decode the musical clues to a character, put yourself in the shoes of the composer, and look at him or her as a storyteller. Constantly ask the composer "Why?" Looking closely at *La Traviata*, one may ask the composer, "Why must Violetta sing for such a long time at the top of her range in the aria 'Sempre libera'?" The answer is a musical clue to her character. In act 2 of the opera, Germont is introduced to Violetta with notes that sound formal and awkward in their articulation and intervals (D downward to F), giving immediate insight into the character. By asking the composer "Why?" one discovers how Verdi, a master of

---

3. Ibid.
4. Frederica von Stade, Interview by author, e-mail, April 2000.

articulation specificity, used the connection or separation of notes and words to provide a musical subtext. Germont's "real" character is revealed by the music.

Which is more important—words or music?

Ideally there should be agreement between the intent of the librettist and that of the composer. Some singers begin with the libretto. For clues to character, singer Franz Grundheber studies the text first, looking to see how the composer was musically inspired by it.[5] Other singers believe that music should have the final say. Bass Kevin Langan says, "Listen to the music in the opera that occurs while your character is singing for clues to what the character is feeling as he delivers the text."[6]

I believe that you should keep an open mind as you look at the text and music for tone, inflection, and other clues that point to the intent of the composer and librettist. Try to be true to the character when you prepare to interpret the role. This means being true to the following:
- Yourself, what you understand
- The composer and librettist
- Historical and cultural context
- Style of the drama
- Relationships with other characters
- Receptivity of the character.

Many professional singers agree that in character preparation the important components are study of the text and music, research, and openness to ideas that come from directors and others. Singer Sally Wolf, known for her detailed characterizations, says, "In general I love to watch people. You can get many ideas from the different 'characters' you see."[7]

On the other hand, Elizabeth Futral goes to the libretto first to "glean clues." She asks herself how the character evolves and looks to discover how the composer has delineated the character. She reads the novel, play, or whatever the source of the opera may be "to further enhance my understanding of the story and the characters."[8]

How essential is research?

Many general character descriptions have been passed on from conductors, directors, and teachers for generations. Often basic characteristics of

5. Franz Grundheber, Interview by author, Indiana University residency, October 1999.
6. Kevin Langan, Interview by author, e-mail, 4 October 1999.
7. Sally Wolf, Interview by author, e-mail, 4 October 1999.
8. Elizabeth Futral, Interview by author, telephone, 22 September 2000.

Meet the Artist: TIMOTHY NOBLE

Timothy Noble is one of the finest singer-actors of our generation. He brings to the stage a commanding, impressive voice with a stage presence and intensity that is astounding. He is known for his attention to the word, to diction, and to molding a multifaceted character. He is celebrated for fully realized fictional characters (Falstaff, Iago, Rigoletto, Horace Tabor, and Amonasro), as well as realistic historical figures (Christopher Columbus and William Tell).

Mr. Noble is also known for his exceptional research into the background of a character. When I met with him, he stressed that research was important but should be used only to round out the human dimension of a character. For instance, Columbus was a rough and tumble man of the sea, but he was from one of the first families to own a library, and he could read. Despite a deeply religious background, Columbus also was responsible for many brutal acts. Mr. Noble feels that these contradictions are the roots of a fully formed character. It is the layers that give the character dramatic range and make the character interesting.[9]

---

well-known roles are documented in books or displayed in videos and live performance. I believe, however, that research into source background materials should stimulate new ideas of character study, not just carry on conventions.

Countless ideas, new and old, are available to the singing actor and director. Just as many different sources inspired the composer to write an opera, many different sources inspire us as we create a character. In some operas it is possible to research the literary work upon which the opera is based for character clues and human dimension. Other operas are set amid historical events or contain historical figures. Still others relate to the culture of a period and chronicle the social and political systems of an era. A brief list of well-known operas, their literary sources, and related research is given in Appendix C.

How do I create a character onstage?

Robert Orth, the baritone who created the title role in Stewart Wallace's biographical opera *Harvey Milk* and Frank Lloyd Wright in Daron Aric Hagen's *Shining Brow*, talks about "using your imagination. That's what it all is—pretending. For me it has the most to do with how true it feels."[10] Orth delineates between "acting like the character" and "being the character." He associates "acting like the character" with a declamatory style of opera acting—eyes unfocused, stock gestures, and not being in the moment: "They're going through the motions without experiencing that character right then." Whereas

---

9. Timothy Noble, Interview by author, Indiana University residency, March 1998.
10. Robert Orth, Interview by author, e-mail, 12 October 1999.

"being the character" requires a singer-actor to step into the character, ready to react to each event as if it is happening for the first time.[11]

But how does one move from "acting like" to "being" a character? One way is to complete a character questionnaire. Although the actions of the character are also important, the questionnaire can help singers explore different facets of their character and serve as a catalyst to further research and discovery. The characteristics revealed through the questionnaire provide a foundation upon which to assemble a character. Subsequent chapters will build upon this analysis. In particular, Chapter 10, "Physical Analysis," provides exercises to ascribe meaning to the actions of your character.

Exercise

4.1 CHARACTER QUESTIONNAIRE

Objective: Establishing basic character guidelines; creating a blueprint of the character.

Directions: Complete the following questionnaire:

Character Questionnaire
Name of opera _____
Character's full name_____Age _____
Place of birth _____

Physical Characteristics:
Height _____ Weight _____
Size description (best word to describe body size) _____
Hair (texture, color, style) _____
Eyes (color, size, description) _____
Facial description (shape of face) _____
Mouth: thin   full
Skin description: pale   dark
Skin quality: smooth   swarthy
Race/nationality _____ Dialect? _____
Marital status _____ Lovers? _____
Education level:
      Not educated in school   Higher degree of education: where?
Economic/social status _____
General physical condition, health, vitality _____
General kinesthetic description (graceful, powerful)_____
Evaluate walk; when is it different?_____
Describe grooming:
            Hair _____   Face _____
            Hands _____   Bathing habits _____

11. Ibid.

Function of clothes — Describe taste in selection and care of clothes _____
Jewelry? _____
What object(s) might you see in the character's hands during the course of the opera?

_____

What item(s) would your character carry in his or her pockets/purse (watch, glasses)

_____

Personality Traits:
In general, is your character a leader, follower, or clown? _____
Does your character have a temper? _____
General Demeanor: Careful/cautious   Bold/chance taker
                         Calm/relaxed   Nervous/anxious
Physical manifestations (biting fingernails, rocking on heels) _____
Other general gestural characteristics (hands in pocket, behind back, etc.)

_____

The Past:
Describe the social/economic conditions under which your character was raised

_____

Work experience _____
Family size _____   Religion _____
Describe your character's mother _____
The father _____
Siblings _____
Your own impression of your character's childhood _____

Relationships:
Describe your character's relationship to other characters in the opera as established;
then in the end _____
What is your character's source of income? _____
Who is your character's best friend? _____
Write out your objectives in each scene in which you appear. What do you want? Does
your character get what he or she wants? _____
Describe your character's reactions to events _____
What is your character's place dramatically in this opera? _____
Your character's place in the drama? _____

Emotional Range:
Circle characteristic emotions of your character:

Amused	Annoyed	Ashamed	Bitter	Candid	Curious
Defiant	Deliberate	Ecstatic	Elated	Enraged	Fearful
Feeble	Forgiving	Frantic	Gentle	Greedy	Hopeful
Impulsive	Jealous	Loving	Meek/timid	Mocking	Nervous
Playful	Pleasant	Proud	Sarcastic	Scornful	Serious
Spiteful	Submissive	Thoughtful	Uneasy	Vexed	Worried

CONCLUSION

Upon first encountering a character, acting teacher Michael Chekhov would always ask, "Is this predominantly a thinking character, a feeling character, or a 'will' character? Is the character's mind slow or quick? Are the feelings passionate or lugubrious? Is the will cold or fiery?"[12] In this way the character moved beyond the opera and became part of a larger community—one filled with thinking, feeling, and strong-willed characters—in other words, people like you and me. To be able to translate a character and come to a deeper understanding of the person, it is helpful to find a way to relate the character to your own experiences. You will always bring pieces of your own personality to the role; it is what makes it uniquely yours.

The detailed study of a particular character should allow the singer to discover something about him- or herself. Similar to rereading a good book, each time we revisit a character, we bring a new perspective and new questions. Each new question allows us to see more deeply into that character. The more choices we have, the more interesting a character can become. A good character study can range from a simple description of the character to a fully formed performance onstage. Most professional singers spend years crafting their characters, and no two singers will approach the task in the same way.

CHECKLIST

- Translate the libretto and note your personal reaction to the text.
- Analyze the music of the character and ask "why" questions about key intervals, dynamics, and musical markings.
- Research the literary and historical sources of the opera to see the elements that inspired the librettist and/or composer.
- Complete the Character Questionnaire so that the physical and emotional makeup of the character is specific. Remember, the history of the character is extremely important.
- Write a short description of the character that answers the following questions:
     1. What does the character want and desire in every scene?
     2. What does the character learn from the beginning of the opera to the end? How does he or she change?

12. Chekhov, *On the Technique of Acting*, p. 161.

3. What clues to the emotions of the character do you find in the text and music?

4. How do you identify with the character? Does the character remind you of someone (in your life or a literary, film, or TV character)?

Environment
Setting the Stage

5

INTRODUCTION

To observe Hermann Prey preparing himself to sing Schubert's "Erlkönig" is to realize that not only is the baritone telling the story, he is also reliving the experience. Like any good storyteller, a singer should not just recall the events—he or she should re-create the atmosphere that brings the words to life. This imaginary ambience stirs and awakens feelings within us that are the essence of our art. The singer-actor needs to "see" the surroundings in order to represent an expanded life, not merely a feeble reproduction of his or her actual environment.

In opera the composer and librettist provide the blueprint for this to occur. From the downbeat of the aria, the specifics of the setting can be made clear on the singer's face and body language. If the actor can articulate what he or she specifically "sees," what memories or visions are being played out in his or her mind, then the audience sees this reflected in the face. When the energy increases to a point at which the actor must sing in order to fulfill an expressive need, the singing actor engages the audience. This rising dynamic of energy and a "need to sing" supplant the waiting of the singer for the entrance.

How can I create an atmosphere of expectation?

A clear and strong focus is essential to creating an atmosphere of expectation. It is direct and does not shift until a thought is completed. Observe in your own conversations with friends how the eyes and focus "work." Even in thought, a friend's gaze will focus on an idea before it is articulated. When someone has something important to say to you and looks directly into your eyes, it is powerful indeed. I am not suggesting that the actor who is singing an aria alone onstage should look into the eyes of the audience. In the performing environment you must imagine a face above the audience—pulling the audience to you. A shift for different phrases gives a division and clarity to your thoughts. Think of this when you are conversing everyday. How can this "reality" be transposed to the stage (see Exercise 3.5)?

Don't I need sets and props to create a specific environment?

No. Try to discover the environment or atmosphere specific to your aria. These discoveries are stimulating and should be utilized whether one is singing in a fully mounted production, or in a rehearsal, competition, or audition. It is particularly useful when auditioning in a new environment to lose oneself in the re-created environment of the scene.

Once the mechanics are finalized, it can be freeing to spend some time exploring the environment of an aria without worrying about vocal mechanics. That is not to say that the voice is ignored. I am simply saying that after so much time is spent working the voice, focusing on the environment or atmosphere can bring new energy and insight to a performance. Deprived of atmosphere, the performance can become mechanical. It is intellectually understood, the singer's technical skill is appreciated, and yet the performance remains cold and heartless.

What is environment?

Ineffable moods and waves of feelings that emanate from one's surroundings
. . . atmosphere.

—*Michael Chekhov*, On the Technique of Acting[1]

The first aspect of environment is the physical elements that can be determined by the notes in the score itself. If you are learning an aria from a compiled publication of arias, the first thing to do is to go to the full score of the opera for a clear description of the setting at the beginning of each scene. Next, examine the scene as you would a historical photograph (see Exercise 5.1): What is the year? Is it indoors or outdoors? What is the time of day? What is the temperature? What objects do you see? What sounds might you hear?

Why is it important to establish an environment?

Once we have thoroughly described the setting, we can open ourselves up to experience the atmosphere. The atmosphere of a gothic cathedral, a hospi-

1 Michael Chekhov, *On the Technique of Acting*, ed. Mel Gordon (New York: HarperCollins, 1991), p. 26.

Meet the Artist: JOHN BERRY

John Berry is currently the Casting Direc-tor and Head of Artistic Administration for the English National Opera (ENO). He has played a central role in the com-pany's development by casting exciting young singers and conductors in new pro-ductions and developing young artists' careers through the ENO Jerwood Young Artists Programme.

Mr. Berry has conducted thousands of auditions. When I asked him what made an audition stand out, he answered, "The singer needs to create his or her own space during the audition."[2] This goes to the heart of the matter. The more specifically created the space, the more realistic it becomes. With "ownership" of this space comes confidence and aware-ness as well.

Mr. Berry suggests that singers open themselves to this creative space and react to it with all of their senses and emotions. In so doing, it will come to life and become real. He notes that so many of these auditions are a vocal demonstra-tion to impress those who listen, with an additional layering of energy and presentational showmanship. "What truly stands out is the singer's understand-ing of the moment at hand, of being inside the music, text, character, and environment."[3]

tal, or a cemetery influences anyone who walks into those spaces. They be-come enveloped in the atmosphere. People also give off a personal atmosphere of tension, hate, love, and fear. All of the above questions and qualities of atmo-sphere are especially important in auditions and competitions when one does not have a director to stimulate the dramatic focus.

Singers often will have more success in auditions and competitions when they sing arias from roles that they have performed in fully staged produc-tions. Yes, the singer has the role in their voice in mechanics and interpreta-tion and the confidence of having performed and communicated the role to an audience as well. But more importantly, the singer has had the advantage of wearing the costume, walking into the sets, and realizing the theatrical at-mosphere created by lighting. When you ask yourself the questions needed to reconstruct the operatic setting, you not only step into the scene, you take the listener with you.

Exercises

5.1 CREATE AN ENVIRONMENT

Objective: Reconstructing a setting.

Directions: Choose a favorite aria and use the following questions to create

2. John Berry, Interview by author, Indiana University residency, November 2001.
3. Ibid.

an environment. Two examples of environments surrounding well-known arias follow.

1. What is the year? Date?
2. Indoors or outdoors?
3. Time of day?
4. Temperature? Is it warm? Chilly?
5. Ventilation? Is it stuffy? Is there a draft?
6. Is it dry? Humid?
7. Describe the lighting. Is it warm? Cool? What are the lighting levels?
8. Describe the smells.
9. How far can you see? Or if you are inside, can you describe the surroundings?
10. Describe in detail elements of your environment. Sketch it out simply. Describe the furniture in detail.
11. Describe all of the parameters of your environment. How many doors and windows? Where are they? Think of a window as a focus when describing something that is seen. Think of the significance of a door through which a loved one has recently passed to the outside or into another room.
12. Are you physically alone in the scene?
13. How does the environment physically and emotionally affect you?

EXAMPLE NO. 1

Act 1, scene 1, *La Bohème*, "Mi chiamano Mimi" (Mimi's aria)

1. About 1830 in Paris.
2. Indoor scene—a garret (a room or unfinished part of a house just under the roof).
3. Late afternoon/early evening with growing darkness and deepening shadows.
4. Temperature—very chilly. It is Christmas Eve (in text). There was some fuel in the stove, but it is long burned out now.
5. Ventilation? It is close to the roof, so most likely it is very drafty.
6. Dry/humid? If you have ever been to Paris in the fall or winter, you will know it to be very humid and damp.
7. Low lighting levels, warm candle glow.
8. It is musty, cigar smell, paint smells from paint and paint-spattered rags.
9. Mimi cannot see very well and walks into a strange environment, but the space is small.

10. Opening description in the piano-vocal score (Schirmer edition):
11. "A large window, with a view of an expanse of snow-covered roofs. A stove, left. A table, a cupboard, a small bookcase, four chairs, an easel, a bed; some books, many bundles of paper, two candlesticks. Center, a door; left another."
12. You are alone with Rodolfo in the scene, though you have heard his friends leave.
13. The environment arouses your curiosity. The furniture and belongings say everything to you about the occupants. A writer lives there, a painter lives there. Books are present. Are they students? Is Rodolfo the painter? Many questions need to be answered. It makes Mimi a little nervous to go into a darkened room alone with someone she doesn't know, but it is also a little exciting. The cold air in the drafty garret makes her cough worse.

Note for environment: It is important to understand Mimi's environment before knocking on Rodolfo's door. She was in her small room alone. Her candle had gone out. It was cold, she was coughing—afraid and lonely.

EXAMPLE NO. 2

Act 4, *Le Nozze di Figaro*, "Deh vieni non tardar" (Susanna's aria)
    1. Mid-eighteenth century.
    2. Act 4 is an outdoor scene.
    3. Late in the evening—all of the action of the opera takes place in one day.
    4. From the growth of the garden of fragrant flowers it could be springtime (see Susanna's text).
    5. It is warm.
    6. Breezes are felt.
    7. Cool lighting of the moonlight creates shadows. Disguises are possible. Mystery is possible.
    8. One can smell the fragrant flowers.
    9. One can see the expansive sky and the stars.
    10. The gardens next to the Count's castle, although one can see (and smell) in the distance pine trees and thick-grown vegetation.
    11. The gardens themselves are "tamed" garden pavilions of bushes. This could even be a maze of bushes to lose oneself in and hide.
    12. It is as important to read the libretto carefully to understand the recitative with the Countess before the aria. Susanna knows that Figaro is "spying" on her, so her aria is for his benefit. She makes his jealousy even more pronounced.

13. The environment has the power to change Susanna's character during the aria—from trying to fool Figaro and play with him to being affected by the environment and being enchanted by it, revealing Susanna's nature as a woman who is in love with Figaro.

5.2 BUILDING A STORY

Objectives: Communicating directly and specifically a story.

Directions: Start to tell a tale very descriptively to those sitting in a tight circle. Pretend you are around a campfire. Those listening will "reflect" the qualities in their own faces. Add color, see it! The story will be passed along in the circle with a question to signal the story "exchange."

5.3 BUILDING THE ATMOSPHERE

Objectives: Making the transition from "telling" to showing.

Directions: A team of three or four members will be given simple weather conditions (storm, sunny, cloudy, rain, . . .) and then asked to verbalize all of the conditions and the emotional qualities the weather condition inspires.

5.4 SETTING AND FUNCTION WITH THE ATMOSPHERE

Objectives: Visualizing the practical applications of environment and describe the atmosphere it invokes.

Directions: A location is announced to all. You decide all of the specific conditions in the make-believe scene. Using the locale, sketch three pieces of furniture. How will you use the furniture? Describe each piece of furniture specifically. What atmosphere will be created by the combination of the locale, conditions, and furniture?

CONCLUSION

The singer is never alone onstage. The environment affects the performer both physically and emotionally. It is a very powerful tool to bring to an audition, competition, rehearsal, or even a song recital. Like a beautifully mounted artwork, the environment provides a frame that showcases the gifts of the performer.

The singing actor should look upon the scenery, costumes, props, and lighting as means to a more powerful performance, not a distraction. Whether these objects are real or imagined, the surroundings can serve as a catalyst to creativity and a bridge between the audience and the singer.

CHECKLIST

- Research the setting of a particular aria.
- Imagine the environment of the scene.
- Answer questions to create a detailed outline of the scene (Exercise 5.1).
- Step into the scene and visualize your surroundings. Describe what you see.
- Write a short description of your scene.

Part II. Integration

Once we understand the parts, we can begin to integrate them into the whole: that is, analysis of movement, the expressiveness of the face, the character, and the environment can be synthesized into planned and improvised movement onstage. To begin, it is important to find a common language with the director and our fellow singing actors as well as to know correct historical styles.

It is also useful to study texts outside the realm of music. Here we can control and create inflection, rhythm, and tempo without formal music construction. Finally, in putting together our character physically from our healthy, neutral posture, we can explore the physical analysis of our character from the outside looking in.

Elements of Stagecraft
Learning the Language

INTRODUCTION

The elements of stagecraft are those accumulated bits of information that are passed on by voice teachers, conductors, directors, books, stage managers, stagehands, and other singers. This includes information we gain from our own experiences—both positive and negative.

This chapter will help singers become familiar with terms heard in the world of opera. Whether it is rehearsal protocol, the roles of the production staff, or equipment utilized onstage, there is a language of the theater. Appendix D offers a detailed explanation of terms and theories that will help acquaint the singer with working on the stage and becoming more comfortable in this environment.

When a singer becomes acquainted with the terminology and skills of stagecraft, it allows him or her to have the confidence necessary to be a true singing actor. Learning the craft of basic stage illusions is crucial to any performer. If a singer becomes concerned about stage business, the anxiety will go directly to their instrument, and the voice may be affected.

What should I do if someone tells me to go upstage?

When you go onstage to perform a role, you are expected to know some basic stage terminology. If the director asks you to move "upstage," you shouldn't have to ask directions. If the stage manager wants you to go to the "center line," then you shouldn't look lost. If you are supposed to "counter" another singer—get moving. Here are some terms that will help you to understand directional terms onstage. A complete list of stage terms is provided in Appendix D.

Up Right	Upstage	Up Left
Stage Right	Center	Stage Left
Enter in "1"		Enter in "1"
Down Right	Downstage	Down Left

AUDIENCE

Above	A stage direction used in describing a position upstage (behind) furniture or scenery.
Below	A stage direction used to indicate a position downstage (in front) of furniture or scenery.
Blackout	Lights are suddenly extinguished on the stage.
Blocking	The rough movements or "traffic patterns" of staging.
Center Line	A line from the center of the playing stage area to the back wall.
Counter	A stage direction indicating that the actor makes an opposing movement (counter) to an actor who makes a cross.
Offstage	Can refer to the wings or away from the center of the stage.
Onstage	Can refer to an entrance onto the stage or toward the center of the stage.

How can I understand what the T.D. and the S.M. are saying?

Sometimes it seems like the technical director (T.D.) and the stage manager (S.M.) speak their own language. They talk easily of "battens" (long horizontal pipes that hang above the stage) and "gobos" (a device that causes patterns of light), "drops" (painted muslin hung at the back of the stage), and "flies" (space above the stage). Most importantly, they expect you to understand what they are saying. Following are some basic stage terms; a full alphabetical listing is given in Appendix D.

Book Flat	Two flats hinged to fold like a book.
Border	A length of painted canvas or other material such as velvet attached to a batten and suspended above the scene to conceal the top of the setting.
Cross-fade	A part of the scene darkens as another brightens.
Cyc	Short for cyclorama: a neutral curtain placed at the back of the stage to give the impression of depth. With the properties of a screen, it can be lit to create atmosphere.

Door Flat   A flat containing a space for a door unit. (It is important to know which way the door opens before rehearsal begins.)

False Proscenium   A semipermanent structure of two wings and a framed border set upstage of the theater proscenium.

Flat   The unit piece of scenery made of painted canvas on a wooden frame.

Fourth Wall   The imaginary wall in the opening of the proscenium arch.

Gel   A plastic filter used to give color to light shining through it. Colors are usually divided into cool light (blue tints) and warm light (amber tints) to show time of day and/or mood.

Practical   A fireplace that has an electric light to simulate a flame or a window that opens is said to be practical.

Scrim   Gauzelike fabric with many uses. It is hung and "flown in" and has properties to be either transparent or opaque depending upon how it is lit.

Teaser   A strip of cloth to hide lighting instruments and hung scenery.

Traps   The trapdoors in the floor of the stage.

What if the director wants me to do an "aside" to a "super" after he has finished his or her "business"?

The shorthand used by a director is important for two reasons. First, stage rehearsals are often planned with time schedule constraints, and the shorthand used by the director expedites matters. This is especially true when there are principals, chorus, and supernumeraries together while a large scene is being staged. Second, when we begin to use the language of the theater we become part of that world. After all, the conductor communicates with musical terms to singers, chorus, and orchestra. Similarly, the director communicates with terms that relate to the dramatic arts.

Aside   Words spoken (or sung) not supposed to be heard by other members of the cast. Designated in the score in parentheses.

Beats   The time between musical phrases in which the actor clearly communicates to the audience a specific emotion.

Business   Actions performed by the actors in pantomime.

Call	Indicates the time to arrive at the theater for costume and/or makeup. A call can also indicate rehearsal ready time.
Character Part	A distinctive role (age, class) of a secondary nature.
Cover	The understudy "covers" the role played by another artist.
Cue	The line of speech or action in the play that is a signal for another artist to begin speaking or an action to be performed.
Going Up!	The stage manager's call warning the company that the curtain will rise in thirty minutes.
Off Book	Memorized.
Prompt	To help an actor by throwing out key opening words or phrases to stimulate the actor's memory. The actor will intone the word "line" when memory fails.
Supers	The supernumeraries engaged for a scene who usually are involved in stage "business" and who do not speak lines. Often they are recruited by the stage manager.

Now that I know what a term means, how do I do it?

Each director has his or her own way of communicating, but many will use the same terms to help you create a powerful performance. It is part of the director's job to give you feedback about how you look and sound onstage. He or she may ask you to "open to the audience" or "feel the light." Although you may understand that "opening to the audience" means turning to the audience, it is often difficult to do this in a natural way. In a similar way, one may understand that to "feel the light" is to have the light shine on your face, but it is often hard to find the light source.

These terms are the tools of your craft—stagecraft. And it takes practice to become a master craftsman. As you go through the exercises, work with a partner or a mirror to see if you are truly following directions.

Exercises

6.1 OPEN TO THE AUDIENCE

Objective: Practicing stage terms: open.

Directions: Also known as "cheating out," opening to the audience places the downstage leg at a diagonal to one of the proscenium corners. This "opens" the body to the fourth wall (audience) and allows the audience a stronger reception to the communicative face, body, and voice.

Meet the Artist: DALE GIRARD

Dale Girard is a well-known combat director and choreographer as well as educator. He has staged fight scenes in the operas *Carmen, Don Giovanni, Faust, Lucia di Lammermoor, Macbeth,* and *Roméo et Juliette* and in many plays. As an educator, he is an advocate for working on effective and safe stagecraft, and in staging hand-to-hand combat, knife, rapier, and dagger techniques, as well as faints, falls, and stage violence. He has taught at Yale University, the Hartt School, the North Carolina School of the Arts, University of Colorado, University of Denver, Harvard University, and the Banff Center. Mr. Girard's workshops have been repeated regularly each summer in the training centers of Central City Opera and Chautauqua Opera.

When I interviewed Mr. Girard, he pointed out that the key to natural-looking faints, falls, and other fight choreography is the musculature and center of gravity: "Remember, all of these routines depend on the illusion of reality, rather than the delicate skeletal framework striking the floor from gravity free-fall." He believes a warm-up is crucial before working through any fight choreography. He then has singers practice step-by-step the

moves that will result in a realistic faint, fall, or fight. He cautions, "Do not expect to be able to do these routines immediately without practice and guidance."[1]

For example, one of the simplest moves is falling to the knees. Dale Girard counsels singers not to "land hard on the knees. Young singers must beware of degenerative knee problems and nails and staples on the stage." He directs singers instead to bend their knees, and as the body begins a forward motion, keep the counterweight of the upper body leaning back slightly: "It is like the old 'limbo' game." In this way the center of weight should be distributed carefully and slowly at first. You can use the feet and ankles for control. To complete the fall, continue the motion to the floor, allowing the feet and legs to slide quickly underneath you. Girard suggests that singers "listen to the floor, with the torso and head." This sideways approach to the floor, with the head turned to the floor, can save a singer's face. Finally, the sound of an impact can be made with the musculature of the arms on the floor, not the bones of the hands. It creates the illusion of a serious fall, without the injury. (See Appendix E for more routines by Dale Girard.)[2]

6.2 CROSS

Objective: Practicing stage terms: cross.

Directions: A cross is a move across the stage for a particular reason. The weight of the body must momentarily shift away from the direction in which the actor is moving onto the leg that is pushing off. If the actor leans in the direction of movement, an awkward crossing of legs will occur.

1. Dale Girard, Interview by author, Indiana University residency, January–February 2001.
2. Ibid.

6.3 PROPS AND FURNITURE

Objective: Working with props.

Directions: Props are not merely for decoration. When in character the actor will remove spectacles for cleaning or hold them in different ways. A fan can be used in countless ways.

Again, furniture is not only for decoration. Try sitting in different ways according to character, or leaning against or walking around furniture according to your character's purpose. Think of how furniture divides the room and affects distance between actors.

6.4 TEXTURE AND PERSPECTIVE

Objective: Using the depth of the stage (texture and perspective).

Directions: Moving onstage left to right without angles looks "flat" from the audience's perspective. Use the depth of the stage for perspective. Think of the meaning of using angles and moving upstage/downstage of your fellow actor. What does it say when the actor turns and moves down or upstage from another actor? How does it empower the actor when the Count in *Le Nozze di Figaro* stays upstage of the Countess or Susanna, circling her, and looking over her shoulder?

6.5 FEEL THE LIGHT

Objective: Finding the light.

Directions: Lighting is an area in which the actor has very little control. The lighting designer and director work together to illuminate the areas in which the staging dictates you will be seen, but sometimes dark scenes create shadows. When the actor holds the head at a certain angle, it is possible to "feel the light" on the face. It is helpful to know where the light source is coming from to find this angle. Is it from the front, from above, or from the side?

6.6 GIVE THE STAGE

Objective: Throwing focus to another person.

Directions: If you are on the same plane, it is not difficult to turn so that the body is facing an angle upstage to the person singing. The body certainly does not always need to be "open" to the audience. The actor who is not singing can listen directly, or can respond according to the "take" or interpretation by turning away, considering what the singing actor is saying, or with body language saying "I do not want to listen." This can take the focus away from the singing actor but is effective when the listening actor is about to sing in response or in a duet.

6.7 TAKE THE STAGE

Objective: Drawing the focus of the audience.

Directions: Take the stage when singing—the eyes of the audience will go to the upstage actor when two or more singers are sharing the stage. The person receiving the focus can find a reason to get to that upstage angle. A cross is in order to consider a thought before responding; backing upstage is a useful stage move when connected with a specific purpose. Always think of action in connection with purpose.

6.8 SUBTEXT

Objective: Developing an inner monologue.

Directions: All moves, especially without singing lines, are made more purposeful with subtext. If you were speaking to yourself under your breath under these conditions, what would you say? If this episode were chronicled in a comic book with the bubble above your head describing your thoughts, what would it say?

CONCLUSION

If singers wish to be considered actors, they must know the vocabulary that is part of the actor's discipline. Singing actors should be able to communicate with the stage director, the assistant director, the stage manager, and each other while working onstage in rehearsal.

Singers should also understand what happens behind the scenes to create the moment onstage. While rehearsing and performing, singers should recognize they are part of a larger community. Many people are responsible for the success onstage—not just the performer.

CHECKLIST

- Study the terms and their definitions.
- Apply the terms to specific actions and objects.
- Develop standard abbreviations of blocking terms so that you can notate your score.
- Become a part of the production community by helping backstage.

Historical Etiquette
Bowing to Tradition

INTRODUCTION

Simply put, the rules of etiquette are the forms described by authority to be observed in social life. Historical etiquette relates to the character and environment of a historical period. Most opera environments chronicle a historical period that includes bows (salutations), walking, and behavior consistent with class divisions. Many operas and plays clearly delineate the social status of the characters, and etiquette often demonstrates the relationship between gender and the classes.

By studying the etiquette of a particular period, a singer not only adds authenticity to his or her performance, but he or she also follows more closely the intent of the composer and librettist. As an ensemble, singers can interact seamlessly if the signals of etiquette are understood. The flick of a fan takes on a deeper meaning when one realizes the historical context. A historically accurate bow highlights the difference between a gentleman and a servant.

In which historical periods are operas set?

Operas have been set in almost every period of history. Most well-known operas are set in the eighteenth and nineteenth centuries. One may think that this is because those two centuries represent the flowering of opera, but composers rarely set an opera in their own time. Often the opera would be set in a slightly earlier time. Designers will often reset an opera in a different, usually later, era to bring a new perspective to the work. Another possibility is the resetting of the opera in the period in which it was written.

Opera Settings: Historical Periods

Medieval and Renaissance	Elizabethan and Restoration	Age of Enlightenment	Romantic
1000–1550	1550–1700	1700–1800	1800–1900
Anna Bolena (Donizetti)	Don Carlos (Verdi)	Un Ballo in Maschera (Verdi)	The Ballad of Baby Doe (Moore)
Le Comte Ory (Rossini)	Don Giovanni (Mozart)	Il Barbiere de Siviglia (Rossini)	The Bartered Bride (Smetena)
Faust (Gounod)	La Gioconda (Ponchielli)	La Cenerentola (Rossini)	La Bohème (Puccini)
Die lustigen Weiber von Windsor and Falstaff (Nicolai/ Verdi)	Lucia di Lammermoor (Donizetti)	Cosí fan tutte (Mozart)	Carmen (Bizet)
Macbeth (Verdi)	Die Meistersinger (Wagner)	Don Pasquale (Donizetti)	L'Elisir d'amore (Donizetti)
Otello (Verdi)	Rigoletto (Verdi)	Die Entführung aus dem Serail (Mozart)	Eugene Onegin (Tchaikovsky)
Roméo et Juliette (Gounod)		Fidelio (Beethoven)	Die Fledermaus (Strauss)
Simon Boccanegra (Verdi)		Der fliegende Holländer (Wagner)	La Périchole (Offenbach)
Tannhäuser (Wagner)		Lakmé (Delibes)	Peter Grimes (Britten)
		L'Italiana in Algeri (Rossini)	Tosca (Puccini)
		Manon Lescaut and Manon (Puccini/ Massenet)	La Traviata (Verdi)
		Martha (Flotow)	Werther (Massenet)
		Mignon (Thomas)	Wozzeck (Berg)
		Le Nozze di Figaro (Mozart)	
		Der Rosenkavalier (Strauss)	

How would I have behaved in medieval times?

Everyone bowed and curtsied (they were called reverences or salutations) upon entering or leaving a room in which there were persons of superior rank. Well-bred persons refrained from indulging in any free, natural laughter, for it was held to be unbecoming and even dangerous, for germs were thought to be airborne. These were superstitious times, and there were recipes for gaining love, fidelity or infidelity, and easy childbirth. Certain jewels were thought to offer luck, protection, or chastity (see Exercises 6.1 and 6.2).

How did customs change during the Elizabethan period?

This was still a superstitious age that believed in magic. The church, since the invention of the printing press, was losing its hold on education. Women would now enjoy certain civic and personal rights, including participation in the more widespread education. Many men and women believed in a greater equality, or at least less inequality, of the sexes. The country of France was ruled by Catherine de Medici, regent for three sons.

Courtship customs decreed that parents choose spouses for their children, who could legally marry at twelve for girls, fourteen for boys. They usually married at about fifteen or sixteen and in their early twenties, and the two were to be within an appropriate rank and status. A betrothal was marked by a gift, often an heirloom, as was Otello's handkerchief given to Desdemona in Verdi's *Otello*.

The men wore various styles of breeches, and the doublet was padded. Capes were draped dashingly over the left shoulder, and heels appeared on shoes and boots after 1558. Men wore their own hair; many were clean-shaven, but others wore small beards and moustaches. Accessories could be swords, canes, daggers, mirrors, gauntlets, purses, muffs, pomanders (apple-shaped caskets containing aromatic substances to "ward off plague" or unpleasant odors), tobacco pouches, and the new, elegant watches.

Women retained the farthingale—cane hoops stitched to the outside of the skirt to maintain its domelike shape—until early in the 1600s. The necessary little gliding steps were somewhat easier when wearing medium heels. Bodices were stiffly boned. Accessories could be fans attached to the waist by a cord, pomanders, handkerchiefs, muffs, lockets, veils, sweet boxes, and masks—the last worn in public to protect the lady's reputation and her complexion.

Hats were worn inside and outside. Ladies wore masks, which were tied with ribbon or mounted on a holder, when attending the theater and in public generally. The glove had to be removed to take an offered hand.

The fan was a weapon of another sort. It could be held, it could be dropped, it could hide, or reveal, draw or repel, attention. It could punctuate a phrase or draw it out lingeringly—altogether a teasing, tantalizing resource. There was an entire pantomime language of the fan, with specific meanings attached to gestures: "We are watched." "Follow me." "I love another." When sleeves were padded, the arm was curved out from the body, and the fan deployed mainly from the wrist. Folding fans came into vogue by 1550.

Dueling was against the law, but it was considered a sign of courage to flout the law. Handclasps were not a form of greeting, but were used as a pledge of friendship or agreement.

People crossed themselves before the altar, at news of death, at mention of witchcraft and plague, and upon sneezing (breath was life). To avert the evil eye they crossed two fingers on one hand, or crossed the two index fingers.

Why were fashions during the Restoration period so elaborate?

The power of France influenced Europe in style and language. England suffered a resurgence of the plague, the Great Fire, and the deposing of James II in 1688. In France the power of the theater was reflected by the works of Corneille and Racine. Form and style were of utmost importance. Racine's style was elegant and simple, with mathematical purity and beauty.

When the English proscription of theater was lifted in 1660, the Restoration stage brought to the theater the proscenium arch, orchestra pit, wings, curtain, lights, scenery, and women actors. Although opera had come with the Renaissance from Italy, its form and style were of the Restoration. A baroque form imported from Italy in the seventeenth and early eighteenth centuries, it reflected the artistic interests of the nobility, in whose houses it had been born.

Exuberance was the word for Restoration fashion. Curls, ribbons, puffs, feathers, ruffles, buckles, bows, furs, and jewelry were attached everywhere on clothing. Elegance and artificiality were sought. Men wore great curled wigs and brimmed and plumed hats or tricornes. Arm movement was restricted by the small amount of fullness at the armholes. Because the upper arms were constricted, most movement was done by the lower arms.

Beards and moustaches were disappearing. Louis XIV of France was clean-shaven. The stiffly boned bodices of the women were tightly laced, and the skirts were heavy and full. In order to sit, a woman allowed a portion of the skirt to move beyond the chair, then stepped back to sit on the chair edge.

Parasols, fans, and masks were worn in public. Patches, muffs, and canes were all accessories. Both sexes wore heels, jewelry, makeup, and patches and sported tall canes. Men wore swords (one should practice sitting while wearing one). A snuffbox was often used. Tapping it saved grains, for snuff was expensive. A pinch is taken with the right hand, and the box lid is closed with the left. One did not sneeze, for that was bad form. Cuffs and shirtfront were then flicked with a handkerchief, as stains were difficult to remove.

How was etiquette simplified during the eighteenth century?

The Age of Enlightenment was a move away from imposing grandeur in favor of light elegance. Art and art criticism were now available to the public.

Men often wore wigs but slowly dispensed with them. Sleeves were more comfortable; coats were knee length and varied in width. Pockets appeared in coats, and heels were low.

Women began the century by affecting a more natural coiffure, with ornaments in the hair. Later elaborate wigs became fashionable. Hoops were out, then in, and became optional in the second half of the century. With hoops, women must walk with small, smooth, gliding steps to keep the hoops under control. Fans reached the height of popularity. Cosmetic spots on the face and black velvet around the throat were accessories.

What was so "romantic" about the Romantic period?

A passionate return to nature, character, soul, and truth and a rejection of rigid form and intellectualization characterized the late eighteenth century. Struggles for intellectual and financial independence, political ideals, and personal happiness imbued the arts and culture of the time. The ideal man was a lovelorn poet and the ideal woman the object of his desire. It was the yearning for the unattainable that created the greatest romance.

Fashion reflected this struggle between desire and duty. Women hid behind veils and scarves. Accessories included muffs, shawls, fans, and gloves. One was taught to be dignified but not proud, elegant but not affected. The growing middle class was becoming a cultural force.

Exercises

7.1 THE MEDIEVAL AND RENAISSANCE MAN'S BOW (C. 1100–1550)

Directions: The right foot is carried to the back, weight remaining forward, and both knees bend. This is a modification of what one would do if one were to kneel. The body inclines slightly forward, head in line with the body, and the hat is removed with the right hand and held at the side, with the inside of the hat hidden. To recover, straighten the body and the front knee, bring the back foot to place, and cover the head.

Costume: long and short tunics with hose, long robes.

7.2 THE MEDIEVAL AND RENAISSANCE WOMAN'S CURTSY (C. 1100–1550)

Directions: Keeping feet and knees together, gently bend knees. The hands can pick up the front of the gown, or they can sweep back with palms forward, an offering gesture. To kiss the hand of the sovereign, the subject kneels, takes the sovereign's hand on the back of subject's own, places the forehead on the back of the royal hand, then stands, bows or curtsies, and backs away.

Costume: Long dresses, often with trains.

The quick "bob" is done by servants and trades people to superiors. It does not elicit a like response. Passing bows are slighter versions of standing bows, used for greeting or acknowledging greetings while walking along a street or making one's way through a throng of guests. To kneel, step back with one foot and sink to the knee. Rise straight up by pushing with the toes of the back foot.

Character Improvisation: Women in ones and twos walk accompanied by relatives or servants. They greet one another in passing, or more formally if they stop to talk. Couples walk together without touching, but if it is necessary to lead a lady the gentleman offers his hand, not his arm.

7.3 ELIZABETHAN MAN'S BOW (1550–1640)

Directions: Bring the left foot back to a comfortable fourth position with the weight remaining on the right leg; at the same time that the right knee bends, the weight then shifts to one's center, both knees bending. At the same time remove the hat with the right hand and incline the body from the waist. The hat can be held at the thigh, the inside hidden. On rising, the weight moves forward to the front leg.

Costume: "Magnificence before comfort." Jerkin, doublets, trunk hose to show calf. Sword a common feature. Capes common for wealthy men.

One can also place the hat under the left arm on the salutation, which would leave the right hand free to make an offering gesture. Take care to place the moving foot to the back, not to slide it, for that suggests a scraping and cringing courtier. The quick bob is done by servants and trades people to one of a higher status, from whom a like response is not called for.

7.4 ELIZABETHAN WOMAN'S CURTSY (1550–1640)

Directions: Draw the left foot back into a slightly open third position. Bend both knees and incline the body slightly. Both heels remain on the floor unless a deep, ceremonious curtsy is called for, in which case the feet would be wider apart and the back heel would come up off the floor. Bows and curtsies in passing are less ceremonious. To greet someone on one's right, turn slightly toward them, and as the right foot takes a step, bend the knee slightly. It amounts to a continuous walk with an acknowledgment in the form of a knee dip.

Character Improvisation: Women with fans signal to men.

Costume: Bodice fit tightly, pointed waistline. Women's skirts swelled outward in domed or drum shapes. Neck ruffles for men and women.

7.5 RESTORATION MAN'S BOW (1660–1700)

Directions: Remove the hat with the right hand, place it in the left hand or under the left arm. Step forward on the right foot (or alternatively place the left foot back) into fourth position, knees turned out. With weight on the front foot, bend the front knee, then shift weight to the back leg and keep both knees bent; incline the body, but both feet remain flat on the floor.

The right arm can sweep forward, down and back, but not past the line of the body. On rising, the hand can be kissed to the one to whom the bow is directed. The weight can remain on the back leg or move forward to the front one. If the hat remains in the right hand, it can be swept back on the bow, with the inside showing. The attitude of the legs was meant to show off a gentleman's fine calf, called "making a leg" in contemporary literature. Menservants, on performing a duty and on leaving a room, bowed the head and body, with heels together.

Costume: Short doublet, petticoat breeches, coat, waistcoat. Sleevecuff (large sleeves).

7.6 RESTORATION WOMAN'S CURTSY (1660–1700)

Directions: With the legs turned out, make a small preliminary step to either side, draw the other foot in to join the heels in first position; bend both knees and incline the body slightly. The hands can remain crossed in front, or let them fall to the sides, or a fan can be held in the right hand. Eyes are lowered, and raised when the knees straighten. If it is to be a deeper curtsy, to show deference to a high personage, come to a fourth position and let the back heel come off the floor. Women servants curtsied (a simple bob) on speaking to employers or any superior.

Costume: Open gown, underskirt.

7.7 EIGHTEENTH-CENTURY MAN'S BOW

Directions: Simplified manners simplified this salutation. The bow could be done either forward or to the side. To bow forward, place either foot to the front and at the same time bend the back knee slightly and incline from the waist. Remove the hat at the beginning of the bow. To recover, straighten body and knee, and shift your weight forward to the leg that first moved.

Costume: Greatcoat, man's suit with trimmed coat, capes.

Alternative bow: Step to either side, bring the free foot to a fourth position back, taking the weight as the knee bends. For a passing bow, the hat was simply lifted; women nodded in acknowledgment. The woman's curtsy remains the same as in the seventeenth century.

7.8 ROMANTIC ERA MAN'S BOW (1800–1900)

Directions: Simplified from previous periods, the bow now consisted only of an inclination from the waist, with heels together, raising the hat with the right hand and letting the arms fall easily to the side. On straightening up, assume the elegant posture for conversing: standing in fourth position with the front knee relaxed. For a more ceremonious bow, begin with a small preliminary step to the side, bring heels together, and proceed as above.

Costume: Trousers, tailcoat.

7.9 ROMANTIC ERA WOMAN'S CURTSY (1800–1900)

Directions: Step to either side, then let the free foot pass behind to fourth position. Bend the knees as the second foot moves, and take the weight onto the back leg. The body and head incline gracefully. Both knees straighten, and the front, weightless, foot is brought in to join the other in a standing position.

CONCLUSION

The knowledge of period etiquette is essential to bringing a character alive onstage. Do your research. To know period modes of behavior, and to have in mind the feel of the costume before the first stage rehearsal is a big advantage for the singing actor. Reproducing gestures and manners that were part of the physical vocabulary of the times lends realism to a character. The style, culture, and customs of a period are of utmost importance in creating believable characters.

CHECKLIST

- Determine the period of an opera or aria.
- Review the etiquette for that period.
- Determine the social status of your character.
- Practice the appropriate bow.
- List some of the rules of etiquette by which your character lives:
    1. How would you greet someone?
    2. What might you wear?
    3. What are the social limits on your behavior?
    4. How does it feel to bow?
    5. What do you look like when you bow?

Improvisation
Unlocking the Imagination

INTRODUCTION

I find that students today have terrific imaginations. However, many subjugate these gifts to the creative model of the composer and librettist and the directives of the conductor, director, voice teacher, and coach. It is often difficult for a student to have a voice as a creative collaborator in opera. That is why an opera workshop should give each singer an opportunity to share his or her creativity with others.

The more a singing actor can stimulate and train his or her imagination, the greater will be his or her power to communicate the depth and meaning of a character onstage. One way to exercise the imagination is to improvise both spoken and sung scenarios. Classroom improvisation exercises even can become a component of performance. Although an essential element of improvisation is freedom, improvisations should always have structure—a beginning, middle, and end. Each improvisation should reflect a balanced dramatic scene and provide insight into dramatic structure.

How do you "break the ice"?

The beginning exercises for improvisation are "icebreakers," designed to be playful and knock down the walls of inhibition that prevent the free flow of acting upon the imagination. Icebreaker exercises (see Exercises 8.1–8.2) draw us out of our shells and free us from our preoccupation with the inhibitions we have in the "real" world. The icebreakers are silly exercises that allow us to enter a fantasy life of our imagination and share that world with others.

Why is improvisation an important tool?

Besides unlocking the imagination, improvisation exercises will help to break down inhibitions. It will help to build a mutually supportive environment, in which students learn to work with each other toward the goal of full interaction onstage. The truly awakened imagination is in constant, fiery motion. Improvisation is not only a training tool. It is a doorway to realism on stage. In life we improvise most of our actions and responses. Improvisation brings this real-life spontaneity to the stage. Improvisation also calls for us to be alive to listening and watching so that we may compose our communications without preprogrammed, rehearsed responses.

Another benefit of improvisation exercises is the recognition of the essential elements of drama itself. While there is still "play," the participants also identify the moments of intensity and elements that are important in all dramatic scenes. The elements are:

- Introduction of characters
- The introduction of the problem and the friction resulting from the opposing forces
- The resolution of the problem and a clear end to the scene (see Exercises 8.4–8.6)

Meet the Artist: HARRY SILVERSTEIN

Harry Silverstein is a popular young director who is noted for his staging at the Chicago Lyric Opera and the opera houses of Houston, Dallas, Seattle, and many other opera centers. He is also involved in training undergraduates at DePaul University in Chicago and has used improvisation as a tool to separate young singers' voices from preconceived ideas of how an opera singer should act. Harry believes that this is a "wrong-headed" notion; there is a difference between singing and acting.

When I spoke with Harry, he explained that when we embark upon improvisation exercises in the classroom, we should aim to have the students open their imaginations and drop preconceptions of conventional opera behavior. If singers are asked to act on an impulse that is familiar—though bizarre—it is amazing how much freer they sing and move without stiffness. Improvisation also allows us to use our imagination in play and frees us from conventions that limit our creative energy.[1]

Sometimes this calls for creating a situation that seems to be outrageous in relationship to the conventions of the aria or scene—for example, Pamina in Mozart's *Die Zauberflöte* is singing "Ach, ich fühl's" while building a sandcastle on the floor; Don Giovanni is singing "Deh vieni alla finestra" while dribbling a basketball; and the Duke in Verdi's *Rigoletto* is singing "Questa o quella" to guys in a locker room (see Exercise 8.17).

---

1. Harry Silverstein, Interview by author, telephone, 17 April 2001.

What is "gibberish"?

Another vocal tool for improvisation is gibberish. Gibberish is the substitution of nonsense syllables for recognizable words. It is a vocal utterance that accompanies an action. When you take away the meaning of the text, clarity becomes dependent upon facial expression and gesture, not word. The singer-actor learns to show and not tell. Body tensions are released, for the body is now a tool of expression. Pantomime will not achieve the same results. Gibberish creates action. Likewise, action creates gibberish. They are interdependent (see Exercises 8.7–8.9).

What is the best way to end an improvisation?

The best way to end an improvisation is to begin with a clear structure. When involved in an improvisation exercise, keep in mind the basic elements of drama when working through an exercise: introduction of characters, the problem, the resolution of the problem, and a satisfying conclusion.

Exercises

8.1 MEISNER'S "RAPID FIRE" STORY[2]

Objective: Freeing the mind, concentration, listening.

Directions: Sitting in a circle, tell a story by having each person in the circle speak one word. Attempt to tell a story "word by word" around the circle. You may want to go around the circle more than once.

8.2 WESLEY BALK'S "SOUND AND MOTION"[3]

Objective: Breaking the ice, interactive awareness, tuning up.

Directions: In a circle each member of the group steps forward one at a time to the center of the circle with a sound and motion on one "beat." It is then repeated by the circle together without a directive "upbeat" preparation. The exercise can begin with sound or motion either played alone or played together simultaneously. The sound/motion can have meaning or can be "off the wall," without meaning (abstract).

8.3 IMAGINATION TUNE-UP

Objective: Affirming uplifting tune-up.

Directions: Introduce a prop. Each person in the circle one at a time will pick up the prop, finding a shape or a meaning to hold it up and say, "This is

---

2. Larry Silverberg, *The Sanford Meisner Approach* (Hanover, N.H.: Smith and Kraus, 2000), p. 7.
3. H. Wesley Balk, *The Complete Singer-Actor,* 2d ed. (Minneapolis: University of Minnesota Press, 1985), p. 116.

a _____." The others in the circle will together say, "What a beautiful _____!"

8.4 CLASSIC MIRROR WARM-UP

Objective: Playing, interaction, body tune-up.

Directions: This is the classic mirror exercise. The two students working together decide who is the mirror and who is looking in the mirror. This can be
exercised full body or just with the face. After a few minutes, change "duties"
to the other student acting as mirror.

Variation: The "twist" occurs in this exercise in step 3 when the two students
exercising together switch from the person looking in the mirror to the person who is the mirror in a manner that is a smooth "handoff." The lead is
taken over back and forth without stopping to agree who will be the mirror
and who will be the person looking into the mirror.[4]

8.5 BASIC IMPROVISATION SCENE

Objective: Introducing play, an important component of the imagination.

Directions: Students are broken up into "teams" of three to five or more. You
may determine the teams by those who are learning scenes together. Write
situations for each team to pantomime (without using the voice) on slips of
paper, and give slips to each team. They are allowed to talk over the setup of
the scene and rehearse for five minutes on their own before presentation.

Do not share the setups with the rest of the class, and introduce the presentation by challenging the students who are watching to determine the situation
after the presentation is completed. Remember the framework of introduction of characters, problem, resolution, and end.

A few sample setups:
1. Family going to a football game
2. Group night out at the opera
3. Going to the grocery store with the children
4. Going to the zoo
5. Nuns at the laundromat.

8.6 BASIC IMPROVISATION SCENE WITH PROP

Objective: Opening imagination and interaction.

Directions: Give a prop to each team (again the team can be those who are
rehearsing a scene). This "prop" can be a recognizable object or not. Each

4. Ibid.

team has five minutes to put together loosely a framework for the improvisation. The voice may be used in this exercise, and each member of the team must handle the "prop" in some manner. Examples of props include broom handles, teacups, a straw, etc.

8.7 BASIC VOCAL IMPROVISATION

Objective: Vocalizing icebreaker, inventive, playful.

Directions: Stand in a circle and pass any musical phrase, known or unknown, to the left. The phrase should end with a question and is answered by the neighbor and in turn passed with a question to the left.

8.8 GIBBERISH 101

Objective: Communicating in gibberish and an icebreaker.

Directions: Stand in a circle; ask a question to the person to your left in gibberish. That person will answer and pass a question to the next person around the circle. Use your usual speech rhythm, let it flow, consider inflection for the difference between the answer and the question.[5]

8.9 GIBBERISH GOES TO SCHOOL

Objective: Communicating, ensemble work, and "thinking on your feet."

Directions: A group of ten decides what kind of school this will be and designates the teacher. The others will be the students. The Where, Who, and What will be decided by the group before the exercise begins. The teacher will lecture, discuss, and interact with the students. All will work in gibberish.[6]

8.10 GIBBERISH AT THE UNITED NATIONS

Objective: Interacting in gibberish, teamwork, ensemble work in gibberish.

Directions: A speech is made by a "diplomat" at the United Nations. A translator stands by to translate after each phrase, both speaking in gibberish. The translator must be sensitive to specific emotions the "diplomat" introduces.[7]

8.11 IMPROVISATION BEHIND THE SCENES

Objective: Improvising in character, building interaction in character.

Directions: Isolate an opera scene that you have learned and rehearsed. Put aside the singing and improvise through the scene, speaking the lines. This

5. Balk, *The Complete Singer-Actor*, p. 147.
6. Viola Spolin, *Improvisation for the Theater*, 3d ed. (Evanston, Ill.: Northwestern University Press, 1999), p. 116.
7. Ibid., p. 117.

is easier to do when accepting that paraphrasing, subtext, and updating will lend sense to the communication.

Take it one step further. Using the example of Mozart's *Così fan tutte* in which Fiordiligi and Dorabella are singing a duet at the opening of act 1, scene 2, go to the "preduet" before the curtain opens. What would the women be saying to each other before the duet? What would happen if they verbalize their thoughts before the duet?

8.12 TRUNCATE IMPROVISATION

Objective: Understanding the Who, What, and Where of the scene.

Directions: Synthesize the entire scene by paraphrasing it in contemporary language. Focus on relationships, the nature of the drama, and the emotions. Use the paraphrased scene as a setup for an improvisation. These spoken improvisations can precede the sung scenes, and they can even be presented in performance before each scene

8.13 SCENE WITHOUT THE VOICE

Objective: Focusing on the energy of the face and body.

Directions: Take away the singing from the scene. Mouth the words. You will find that you will make eye contact more frequently with those onstage, reliant on lip reading for cues rather than auditory clues. In this exercise we must "show" without the use of our voice.

8.14 IMPROVISATION WITH DIFFERENT TEMPI

Objective: Isolating a tempo character by character.

Directions: The leader will direct tempi on both sides of a fast-food counter —servers and customers. Make very clear distinctions between those servers who are experienced and nonexperienced, motivated and not motivated. Develop a thumbnail sketch to explain the tempo of each character. On the other side of the counter some customers are in a hurry, others are not. Some have children. Some are older, some younger.

Variations: Waiting in line at a bank; waiting in a supermarket checkout line.

8.15 PLAYING TOGETHER WITH TEMPO

Objective: Building sensitivity to each other's tempo in scene work.

Directions: Two or more players agree on the Who, What, and Where for a scene in "real time." The scene is then repeated in slow motion, and then repeated in a fast tempo.

8.16 SLOOOOOOOOOW MOTION FREEZE TAG

Objective: Learning the difference in the body between slow movement and slow motion in improvised movements within the game.

Directions: The leader chooses the first "it." All players run, dodge, and breathe in slow motion. When tagged the person freezes in a sustained statue before tagging the next person. On tagging the next "it," the person who tags freezes until the game is over.

This last tempo exercise is playing with the tempo and varying speeds within the opera scene itself.[8]

8.17 IMPROVISING THE OPERA SCENE WITH TEMPI PLAY

Objective: Playing within the scene at differing time frames, which the singing actor will perform on the stage.

Directions: Work a well-rehearsed opera scene at varying tempi. The control will come from the pianist, ranging between slow motion/sustain (freeze) and presto.

8.18 IMPROVISING THE CHARACTERS

Objective: Understanding the character's personal makeup by placing the character in an "out of context" setting.

Directions: While the singers are working on an opera character in a scene, assign them an improvisation that places the scene in a new context.

Examples:
- Musetta and Marcello visit a marriage counselor (Don Alfonso).
- Infomercial on TV. Iago is selling a boat.
- Belmonte has returned from Turkey and becomes a minister. He delivers his first sermon, entitled "Jealousy and Forgiveness."

8.19 TRUST EXERCISE I

Objective: Building physical trust within the class.

Directions: Divide the class into groups of five or six. One person will be in the middle of a tight circle. Have them close their eyes, and, with the arms at their side, let the body go off balance. The person in the middle must depend on the members of the tight circle to "catch" them at the shoulders.

8. Ibid., p. 213.

8.20 TRUST EXERCISE II

Objective: Building physical trust within the class.

Directions: Break the class up into pairs. One person will close their eyes and allow themselves to be guided around the room. They can even go outside the classroom if the instructor allows. Each pair will take a "vow" that the leader will keep the follower safe, and that the follower will not open their eyes.

CONCLUSION

Improvisation exercises add new layers to characterizations and play with the interaction between characters. Improvisation provides different perspectives on a scene and exposes the dramatic structure of a scene. Improvisation releases tension and focuses on the process rather than the product of rehearsal. However, improvisation should never be a free-for-all. It is most useful when it has structure and purpose.

Everyone has the capacity to be imaginative and creative through improvisation. However, we often need permission to act on our creative impulses. This is often not encouraged in the product-driven environment of opera performance. When we begin to use our imagination, we are on the road to unlimited possibilities for a character, making our stage work interesting, varied, and—most of all—exciting.

CHECKLIST

- Break the ice and drop judgment.
- Be open to playing with scenes, characters, and voice.
- Look at props and settings in new ways.
- Free the voice with gibberish.
- Communicate without the voice.
- Play with movement and tempo.
- Trust yourself and others.
- Before you begin an improvisation, write down your plan. When you have finished the improvisation, write down what you actually did. Compare the two. Why did you make the choices you did "in the moment"?

Monologues
Talking Opera

INTRODUCTION

The practice of spoken monologues in opera workshops can be of value on many levels. First, the singer has spoken lines in musical theater and operetta. Second, the singer will also have dialogue in a number of standard works, including *Die Zauberflöte*, *Die Fledermaus* (J. Strauss), *Manon* (Massenet), and the original opéra comique version of *Carmen* (Bizet). Finally, dramatic monologues can give the singer insight into their operatic equivalent—arias.

Through exercises, singers can learn to project without forcing their speaking voices. When we tighten the voice and body trying to project, the result is "opera speak," or an artificial and false reading.

Why should I learn a spoken monologue if I am a singer?

The practice of rehearsing spoken monologues in workshops will focus the singer's attention on the text and the expression that comes from rhythm, inflection, and coloring the words. There is a sense of artistic freedom that comes from the realization that the speaker literally creates the "musical pattern in the phrase." While the composer has this power in writing music, the speaker has a choice over every breath, pause (dramatic beat), rhythm, inflection, and dynamic of the text.

In addition, the importance of learning an appropriate monologue is becoming more important to the young singer because many intern and training programs now require a monologue in the audition package.

Where can I find a monologue?

There are over five hundred different collections of monologues from plays currently in print. Most libraries have collections of monologues in the drama section. You can also go to the Internet and go to a site that sells books, like Amazon or Barnes and Noble or even a used-book site. Type "monologue" in the search box and see which book suits you.

What should I look for in finding a monologue that suits me?

There are two main types of monologues: a "ladder," in which the speech steadily builds to a climax, and a "stepping stone," in which the speech travels emotional peaks and valleys. Professor Ann Woodworth of the Northwestern University School of Speech and Theater suggests that you search for a monologue that contains some kind of transition for the character. The emotional character at the beginning of the piece should be different from the emotional character at the end. In a two-minute piece, singers should look for material that allows them to make an emotional change within the first fifteen seconds and three or four times again before the end.[1]

What is the best way to memorize a monologue?

It is often not easy for singers to memorize monologues. The vocalist is accustomed to attaching words to a particular pitch and rhythm value. Take that away, and we lose our compass. Try to speak your text from an aria without the music, and you will see what I mean. The best way to memorize your monologue is to find the way in which you memorize things in your daily life. Do you write things down? Do you need to say it aloud? Do you need to see it to memorize it?

Some people break a monologue down into several sections. Key words may remind you of how each section begins. In memorizing each sentence there will be important words that will stick in your brain, rather than your trying to memorize word for word. Get accustomed to speaking the words aloud to feel the words in your mouth.

After memorizing the entire monologue, begin to play with inflection and all the values that we know as musicians (dynamics, rhythm and tempo, color). Enjoy the freedom that the actor has in not having to adhere to the composer's directions.

Is it important to know the context of a monologue?

Professor Woodworth finds that "one of the biggest problems with monologues is that students often forget they are still in a dialogue even though the

1. Ann Woodworth, Interview by author, e-mail, 2 January 2001.

Meet the Artist: JUDY NUNN

Judy Nunn is a professional actress who works with singers. Judy is married to the baritone Brian Nomura, who is especially noted for his Lieder interpretations. When Judy works with young singers, she is aware that few have found monologue material that is appropriate to them at this point of their development. She feels that it is important for the young singer to have an accurate sense of him- or herself when choosing a monologue. Find a character that is stage-appropriate for a college student, not a mature professional. Also, it may be ill advised for a young singer-actor to take on a monologue for a much older person.[2]

Judy helps the students focus on what they (the characters) want in the monologue. What is the intent of the scene? What do you want, and from whom do you want it? Moreover, to whom are you speaking? "To create a strong dramatic impulse, your choices are very important. To intensify the impulse, make a strong choice." Just talking with "a friend" is not a strong dramatic choice; arguing with an estranged lover is.[3]

She advises that when the rhythms of the monologue become dry, shake it up a little: try it with an accent, perhaps a Southern, Italian, or New York accent. The accent does not have to be proficient to change the cadence. Change the sounds. Change the inflections to show how that changes meaning, emphasizing different words and syllables. Try different vocal colors, long pauses, and different breathing points. See the difference between "sharing your voice with the audience" and "under the breath to yourself."[4]

---

actor is the only one speaking." She points out that it is easy for the speech to sound prepared or static because the actor loses a sense of intention, or purpose: "Sometimes I will have the actor paraphrase the speech, put it in his or her own words." Other times Professor Woodworth will have the actor speak directly to another actor, often asking the second actor to vocalize responses or ad lib lines: "Usually I am just trying to help them find what is active about the speech, what is dramatic."[5]

Even when you are the only one onstage during a monologue, you are not really alone. You are always communicating with someone. Try to treat every monologue as a two-character scene. Identify or invent strong, clear, or concrete goals for your character. To whom are you speaking? Perhaps the other person is *not* sympathetic to your needs and desires. This is a conflict. This other character may walk out on you, mock you, or interrupt you. This character could be very important to you. They may have an opinion you respect. The energy of this communication, thinking through the strategy of trying to

2. Judy Nunn, Interview by author, telephone, February 2000.
3. Ibid.
4. Ibid.
5. Woodworth, interview.

gain something or convince someone, is the impulse that provides the dramatic spark.

How should I begin my monologue?

The beginning is extremely important. Ask yourself, "Where does the vitality or urgency come from?" Without spending a great amount of time, find a personal "trigger" for your emotional commitment to the character. A trigger, such as a song, can link an emotional response to a memory. Replay a scenario in your mind. Find a key word or image that occurs in everyday life.

How should I practice my monologue?

Robyn Hunt of the University of Washington suggests that you "work very diligently on uncovering the given circumstances for your character. Read the play for these givens, and read it several times with full attention. Be clear about the character's relationship with the listener." She insists that her students know why the character must speak at this moment in the play, and to what end. She asks that they clarify the distance the listener sits (or stands) from the character, and why. Students practice aiming for, and turning away from, this location with ease and naturalness, being able to return to it after looking away for a thought or a recollection.[6]

Evan Yionoulis, Chairperson of the Yale School of Drama, also suggests that singer and actors begin by reading the play carefully for clues to the given circumstances: "Ask who the character is, when and where the scene takes place, what just happened, who the character is talking to (could be the audience), and what he or she wants from them (the character's objective)." He points out that there is always the additional challenge of having to "posit the listener's response and of choosing where to put your focus in the audition room."[7] An important new resource for the study and practice of monologue delivery is *The Monologue Audition: A Practical Guide for Actors*, by Karen Kohlhaas.[8]

Are there monologues in opera?

Yes! They are called arias. Arias reveal emotions and recount experiences, dreams, and history. The composer, of course, dictates the structure of the monologue and tells you where the sections are (e.g., where the emotional high point comes). Note the placements of decisions and transitions in text,

6. Robyn Hunt, Interview by author, e-mail, 27 November 2000.
7. Evan Yionoulis, Interview by author, e-mail, 22 January 2001.
8. Karen Kohlhaas, *The Monologue Audition: A Practical Guide for Actors* (New York: Limelight, 2000).

which is reflected in the music. One of the difficulties that singers have as they transition from singing to speaking onstage is that they feel that their vocal production must always be the same. Although the spoken voice in an auditorium must always be supported and focused, there are ways to exercise spoken communication in such a way that the spoken voice is heard—and understood, and yet the delivery is not forced.

Exercises

9.1 OPERA SPEAK OR NOT OPERA SPEAK

Objective: Playing with inflection and projection in dialogue.

Directions:

Step 1: Take the following oration from *Die Zauberflöte* for a male and speak it with as much majestic power and resonance as you can muster:

> Devoted servants of the temple of wisdom: I declare that today's assembly is one of the most important of our time. Tamino, a prince, waits at the portal of this temple, longing for the enlightenment toward which all of us have been striving with energy and zeal. To watch over this high-minded youth, to extend to him the hand of friendship, will be our noblest duty.[9]

Step 2: Take the same speech and speak it in conversational tone.
Step 3: Combine steps 1 and 2 by emphasizing important syllables and projecting those words with resonance, but without pushing. Use the device of pausing a beat to underline the text. Hear the difference at the end of a line between an upward and downward inflection.

9.2 OPERA SPEAK II

Objective: Playing with focus shifts.

Directions: Take the following selection from *Die Zauberflöte* for Pamina and speak it with the indicated focus shifts:

> Oh, Tamino, here you are! I heard the sound of your flute and followed its tone as swift as an arrow . . . but you are sad . . . Speak to me, my love! Don't you love me any more? Papageno, please tell me what troubles my Tamino. (Papageno is silent.) You, too? Oh, this is worse than death! (This text is followed by the aria "Ach, ich fühl's.")[10]

Pamina's speech is difficult to manage without melodramatic indication of emotion. Keep in mind the importance of focus on three different areas.

---

9. Translation by author.
10. Ibid.

One area is Tamino, the other is Papageno. The third area can be a focus area to which "this is worse than death" is directed. There is a distinct difference between Pamina's joy at having found Tamino and the despair that follows. Think of the dramatic beats (pauses) that are important in building intensity.

Inflection is important. See how the meaning changes by changing the stress on syllables each time you speak the lines. Make choices of specific emotional attitudes for each phrase. They need to be clearly defined and specific for maximum strength.

CONCLUSION

In many ways, the processing and performance of the monologue can be equated with musical values. However, in the actual vocal production, there are times in which a singer is trying to produce a large spoken sound and pushes the sound, causing it to sound artificial. By focusing the words forward and using the lips and tongue to intensify important words, projection is naturally produced without tension. Onstage the vocal production behind "talking" opera is as important as that behind singing.

In addition, monologues are now an important part of the "package" young singers need for major auditions. Besides its inclusion into the audition package, learning how to deliver a monologue from "straight theater" is an important skill. In a spoken monologue our focus goes to the intention, needs, and communication of the character. In essence, we are composing our own music as we recite the text.

CHECKLIST

- Choose a monologue.
- Read the monologue through and memorize it.
- Play with inflection and tone in the monologue.
- Focus on those to whom you are presenting the audition.
- Be aware of your vocal technique as you speak.
- Find the monologues in operas.
- Practice moving between singing and speaking.
- Write down how you feel when you speak an aria as opposed to singing it.
    1. How do you feel physically?
    2. How do you feel emotionally?
    3. What did you discover about the aria?

Physical Analysis
Moving in Character

10

INTRODUCTION

A player can dissect, analyze, intellectualize, or develop a valuable case history for a part, but if one is unable to assimilate it and communicate it physically, it is useless within the theater form. It neither frees the feet nor brings the fire of inspiration to the eyes of those in the audience.

— *Edwin C. White and Marguerite Battye,* Acting and Stage Movement[1]

An important learning tool of physical character application is daily observation in life and practice. If you really take the time to look, each person has a specific physical makeup that reveals something about him or her.

Body language can tell you if a person is extroverted or introverted, happy or sad, an indoor person or an outdoor person. Some people use their hands to communicate; others do not. Watch for mannerisms that are repeated. Use what you observe to build a realistic characterization.

How do people move differently as they age?

As a person approaches middle age, he or she might observe a stiffness of movement in their legs and arms, and especially a reduction in the ease with which younger people can turn the head. Younger people move with quicker movements. As one ages there is more caution in movement. In the hands of the young, fingers are usually spread—touching objects for balance. They have restless hands that move quickly, rub eyes, point, and push hair out of their eyes.

1. Edwin C. White and Marguerite Battye, *Acting and Stage Movement* (Colorado Springs, Colo.: Meriwether, 1985), p. 65.

The following list describes some general characteristics of middle and old age:

- Feet and knees turn outwards (when seated, too).
- Women sit knees apart; men sit with their knees together.
- Knee joints are rigid. Movement is from the knees, not the hips.
- On lowering to a seated position, the trunk is thrown forward.
- Middle-aged hands show characteristics of culture, sophistication (turn of the wrists, fingers together).
- Elderly hands show uncertainty. The fingers are spread and fumbling.

What is a "characteristic gesture"?

A characteristic gesture is one that can be used throughout the opera for the character—a movement characteristic of the person's station, state of mind, and body language. It is often as personal as a signature. For example, a periodic hand through the hair while thinking the same way each time will personalize the gesture.

When putting on a garment, a youth would bring it over the head with arms raised in order to place them in the sleeves instead of moving them downward through the sleeves (e.g., Cherubino in *Le Nozze di Figaro*). When a youth is seated, his or her arms do not come to their sides. The elbows are away from the body. A young child would swing their arms when walking, less so during adolescence. In general, youthful movement is self-conscious and awkward in turns.

On the other hand, in middle age the arms would be held closer to body with the hands possibly in the pockets. In old age there is restricted movement from the elbows. One would bend at the hips, and the shoulder girdle is rigid. In general, young or old, the vitality wanes during fatigue, illness, and shock.

What is the relationship between the character and movement onstage?

Judy Yordon, in her book *Roles in Interpretation*, suggests that singers "let body traits come from your knowing who the character is and how that character will respond."[2] Singers can use Who, What, Where, When, and Why questions to explore a character's circumstances. Who is the character in society? What is the character wearing? Where is the character? When is the character living? Why is the character moving? The world surrounding the character and their interaction with that world affect how the character will move.

2. Judy Yordon, *Roles in Interpretation* (Boston: McGraw-Hill, 2002), p. 197.

Meet the Artist: SUSANNE MENTZER

American mezzo-soprano Susanne Mentzer is best known for her portrayals of the *travesti* parts (Italian for "pants" or "trouser" roles) of the lyric repertory: Cherubino (*Le Nozze di Figaro*), Idamante (Mozart's *Idomeneo*), Sextus (Mozart's *Clemenza di Tito*), Octavian (Richard Strauss's *Der Rosenkavalier*), and the Composer (Strauss's *Ariadne auf Naxos*).

Ms. Mentzer has seen her characterization of Cherubino evolve over the years. She is a very reactive performer.

She tries not to analyze too much the individual physical characteristics because it makes her feel stiff and self-conscious. Although she has analyzed the inside and outside of the character, she feels that the frame of mind is very important: "If I think masculine, I become masculine." To make each production interesting she often waits to see how others in the cast conceive their roles, and thus finds different reactions and characterizations (and fresh ones) with each cast.[3]

When opera singer Frederica von Stade tries to assimilate movements given to her by directors, she writes down the movements in her score: "I put a meaning to it so that I can remember it." Rather than an exhaustive analysis of the character, she uses the meaning of the gesture and movement to memorize her stage blocking: "I do need a reason, even a ridiculous one, to remember a movement or a gesture, or I'll never remember it."[4]

Affective memory of movement is also important—not only analyzing what you have observed in others, but remembering a time in your life when you have experienced a similar situation. In the article "Stanislavsky and the Classical Singer," author Experience Brian relates how Stanislavsky would have actors use the magic "If." If I were Mimi in Puccini's *La Bohème*—If I were hungry and ill, how would I move? If I were shy, if I met a young man and was stimulated by this contact, how would I behave? How would I move? What would I do, and how would I do it?[5]

Stanislavsky recommends that the singer, before entering in character, create a moment before the entrance. Tamino's entrance in the opening of *Die Zauberflöte* is an excellent example. If you wait for a cue and simply run out onstage pretending to be scared, it will look artificial. Stanislavsky drew a distinction between physical movement, which is a mechanical act, and physical action, which has some reason for happening—an inner justification. Do not act "as if you were doing, for this is only showing, indicating, and

---

3. Susanne Mentzer, Interview by author, e-mail, 19 September 2000.
4. Frederica von Stade, Interview by author, e-mail, April 2000.
5. Experience Brian, "Stanislavsky and the Classical Singer," *Classical Singer Magazine*, October 2000.

exhibiting. An action is first internal [intention] and then external [action]. Every operatic character has an intention and action at all times."[6]

Can props help me to move in character?

Yes! Jerold Siena has sung extensively at the New York City Opera and in a variety of roles at the Metropolitan Opera. For an elderly character, Mr. Siena chooses one predominant physical characteristic to build around. It is the makeup in rehearsal and performance that makes him feel old: "I love to have a prop in my hand. I always find a way to use it so that it reinforces my character and the central ideal of that particular scene." He likes to use models from real life. For the Captain in Alban Berg's *Wozzeck* he thought of Mussolini, and as Basilio in *Le Nozze di Figaro* he wore a donkey skin that made him feel like the detective Columbo with his raincoat. Mr. Siena feels that it is important to fully prepare first: "Fill yourself with facts as you prepare, then let it go!"[7]

What should my face be doing?

To create a young character, the eyes would be wide open and unblinking when attention is held. You should stare steadily before moving to the next in more rapid focus changes. The mouth is relaxed, not tense, and reflects the lack of concentration of youth. As the character ages, the emotional content is higher. The mouth is harmonized with the body. As tension increases in the body, the mouth tightens and purses. In old age the face pulls down. The eyes peer in a struggle to focus. The adjustment in focus between near and faraway objects is evident.

Exercises

10.1 AT THE ZOO

Objectives: Taking on the physicality "from the outside" of an animal.

Directions: Each person takes the "role" of an assigned animal. If possible, observe the animal and reproduce specifically, not generally, its movements, and include the shape of the spine, the tempo of the personality, and even the shape of the head.

10.2 PHYSICAL EXAGGERATION

Objective: Developing a consistent characteristic gesture through exaggeration.

Directions: Place four people on chairs in a line representing a number of

6. Ibid.
7. Jerold Siena, Interview by author, e-mail, 18 September 2000.

persons waiting to audition. Each should select one gesture that shows irritation or nervousness and repeat it over and over again. Some suggestions:

- Sweaty nosepiece on the eyeglasses
- Dirty eyeglasses
- Stiff neck
- Teeth and jaw tension
- Sweaty palms
- Dandruff problem

10.3 MOVEMENTS WITH A MESSAGE

Objective: Imbuing abstract movements with purpose, inner power, and awakened activity.

Directions: Make abstract movements with your hands, arms, legs, and feet, and finally, with your whole body. Each movement must leave an outline in your surroundings. Muscular tension is not desirable. The movements should be broad, full, and clearly differentiated from one another. Do the movements in different tempi with different intensities.

Variation: Try the same exercise with flowing movements. Each movement should be slurred into another in an unbroken line.

Variation: Add singing to the same movements.

10.4 RADIATING PHYSICAL FOCUS

Objective: Freeing physical tension by radiating out a focused physical intensity.

Directions: Imagine that invisible rays stream from your movements into space, in the direction of the movement itself. Send out these rays from your chest, arms and hands, and your whole body. Allow the articulation of the movements themselves to be varied.

Variation: Add singing to the exercise.

10.5 FINDING THE WALK

Objective: Observing and playing with characteristic walks.

Directions: Observe a distinctive walk of someone you see on the street or in film or television. Be prepared to discuss the character and relationship to the walk. A walk can reveal the age, the tempo of the personality, the will, or his or her inner passions.

10.6 RELATIONSHIP BETWEEN BODY AND EMOTION

Objective: Observing subtle physical alterations during sustained emotion.

Directions: Choose an emotional quality with a strong focus (e.g., anger). Make subtle physical alterations and sustain them. Lower your head and look downward. How does this affect the emotion? Turn your palms away from you. Incline your head on one side. Slightly bend the knee of one of your legs. Observe how every subtle sustained alteration of movement can subtly change the emotion.

10.7 IMAGINARY BODY

Objective: Observing how powerful mental suggestion affects physical characteristics.

Directions: First provide the psychological profile of the character, then add the imaginary body (gestures, physical characteristics). After you have created a psychological profile (see the example), ask yourself the following questions: What would you look like? What characteristic gestures might you have? How would you walk? How would you physically interact with specific characters?

Example: You are King Philip II of Spain. You have ruled for many years and are thought to be a strong and mighty ruler. Your son, Carlos, will someday be king, but you worry about him. He is idealistic, headstrong, and foolhardy.

You also worry about your wife, Elisabeth. Yours was an arranged marriage for the sake of peace. You love her but do not trust her. You can confide in very few people. You must always appear to be a strong and unbending ruler, but the crown is wearing you down. There is another threat—the Grand Inquisitor. The power of the church is a mysterious force with which to be reckoned. You want to lead your people, to be respected and loved, and for your son to follow your example.

CONCLUSION

Just as no two people show their age in the same way, so is each character unique. In the final analysis, let the music, text, and story assist you. Physical character is a practiced craft that comes from study, exercise, and experience. The more precise you are, the clearer the physical fingerprint.

In the final analysis we must take several steps offstage before we step onstage. We must think about the specific physical characteristics—practicing walks, facial mannerisms, and gestures without the music. We must coordinate the physical characteristics with the vocal demands of the role. Finally, we must integrate all these elements into a three-dimensional characterization. Only then are we ready to walk onstage.

CHECKLIST

- Ask yourself the following questions:
    1. What am I doing?
    2. Why am I doing it?
    3. How am I doing it?
- Physically analyze your character.
- Observe the physical differences around you of type, including age, gender, height and weight, infirmities, even metabolism.
- Practice by looking into a mirror.
- Describe what you see in writing.

Part III. Application

A powerful performance, whether it is in the context of a fully staged opera, an audition, a competition, or even a recital, has to do with the projection of energy without tension, a full understanding of the moment, and a clear and specific idea of what you want to "say" and how you want to "say it." The tools of voice, body, and face should be utilized to engage the audience. The performance becomes a synthesis of all that a singer needs to express at that moment.

To this end, "play" in practice can be useful. Many preconceptions of character and music are rigid. Play allows us to experiment, break down the walls, and see that many choices are possible. Play also puts us in touch with our inner child. This child is imaginative, uninhibited without self-consciousness, and brings a "can-do" attitude to the creative process. In addition, the intent of the composer and shape of a scene or aria are explored, with "dramatic hinges" playing an important part.

As singers prepare to move from the workshop into the real world, they are introduced to several perspectives outlining the expectations of composers, directors, conductors, and coaches. They explore the realities of performance anxiety, and they make important decisions about their careers.

The Aria
Making Choices

INTRODUCTION

In opera arias lie opportunities for the singer to connect with the audience. Arias give us a chance to communicate directly with the audience in a very personal way. To "open up" and break down the barriers between audience and performer, singers can focus on an emotion that they wish the audience to also experience. It means fully engaging the audience—distilling a moment and suspending time.

In an interview Håkan Hagegård, noted opera and Lieder performer, told me that "the more intimate the form of performing, the closer to the center of creativity the re-creating performer can come." He pointed out that as a singer moves closer to the creative center of words and music, less grand gestures are needed: "When you think the 'right thoughts' and are in tune with the work, you don't have to 'do' so much."[1] Unfortunately, in opera arias, unlike Lieder singing, we often stray from this center. I recommend that, whenever possible, artists practice in their native language. Most likely it is the language that will reflect their thought processes and emotional center.

How does an aria capture a "moment in time"?

When done well, an aria can slow and even suspend time as audience and singer share "the moment." In the aria "Deh vieni non tardar" from *Le Nozze di Figaro*, Susanna pauses to reflect as all of the disguises and plots are revealed in this "moment of truth." All is quiet before the storm of the act 4

---

1. Håkan Hagegård, Interview by author, e-mail, 13 January 2001.

finale. She gazes up at the night sky filled with stars. She tilts her head to feel the breeze, and she turns to listen to the murmuring brook. In other words, all of her senses are engaged as she experiences "the moment." To join her, the audience must follow her focus and experience it with her (see Chapter 3).

A similar set of observations takes place in "Ain't it a pretty night" from the opera *Susannah* by Carlisle Floyd. There is no way that Susannah can take in all of the stars in one glance. Awed by the sight of so many stars, she will look at specific stars for varying brightness, at constellations, and scan the sky.

Sometimes the physical environment is less important than the social environment. Many arias have a tone of pleading or trying to persuade. An exercise we use for Liu in Puccini's *Turandot* has her taking a step toward another singer while she is singing "Signore, ascolta." She pleads with the face only for a line and one thought at a time. The singer listening has the choice to look away or to engage the gaze. Then Liu must find another person to sing to and convince with her face, body language, and commitment to each moment. In every aria there is a kernel of the thought process of the character. It is often either a physical observation, a reminiscence, or singing directly to another person onstage.

How might the intent of an aria affect my focus?

A very important determinant of the focus is the intent of the singer. This can be the overall intent of an aria or the specific intent of a phrase. The overall intent of Musetta singing "Quando m'en vo'" in the second act of Puccini's *La Bohème* can be said to be the desire to seduce Marcello after attracting his attention. An effective exercise has Marcello sitting while Musetta steps toward him, commands his attention, and tortures him in any number of ways. Besides Marcello, she is also playing to the crowd, making Marcello jealous, and embarrassing Alcindoro. Other dramatic "beats" can be slyly looking for his reactions and even frustration that her intentions are not immediately received. Each specific intent is important.

How much should I use gestures during my aria?

An involuntary movement of hands or arms during difficult vocal passages can signal tension in the body, especially when the arms feel as if they are shortening into the shoulders and neck. If you feel moved to gesture, then let go and do it! Rather than going halfway, commit to the gesture and sustain it. When a pattern of gesture is repeated over and over, it can be distracting and predictable, becoming a cliché.

A recent study by Jana Iverson, professor of psychology at the University of

Missouri, reveals that gestures have been found to be helpful to the thought process as the mind searches for words in the communication process.[2] For singers, coordinating a gesture with the words in an aria has always been a difficult task. By remembering that the gesture helps with the communication of words, you can time your gestures appropriately.

What if I feel myself getting tense during an aria?

Tension in the shoulders and neck can be released by increased use of the legs and core support. Be aware of the strength of the leg muscles and engage them, lengthening the spine at the same time. Realizing the bone mass weight of the arms and not allowing them to be pulled in and "held" is helpful. Feel the weight of arms and let them hang. This will help the shoulder girdle to remain in a low, natural position.

If a singer is holding tension in the arms, a simple test is to walk to the singer's side while they are singing and lift the singer's arm. Then let go. Often the arm will remain in space when tension is present. If the arm simply falls to their side, the upper body is freed from tension. The instructor may also place a hand on the back of the singer during the aria to remind the student to stretch in the back, or rest a hand gently on the shoulder as a reminder to release shoulder tension. Always make sure that the knees are released and not locked.

Singers are trained in the studio to avoid any hand or body movement that would be distracting to an audience. But some of this movement is unconscious release of tension, and when the singer is forced to be still and the stance is intended to form a base of strength and stability, the singer can become rigid and "locked" in that stance. Another expression that can be unfortunate is to "plant yourself." In this case there will be a loss of flexibility, balance, and ease of vocal production.

The sense of tension release is especially evident when the singer is in a physical and mental attitude of readiness—the student has the balance to move in any direction at any time. A good example is a cat at rest. The cat in repose can still move quickly in any direction, with strength and purpose. Another useful exercise to demonstrate to the student the difference between tension and release is to invent two simple signals before the student sings. One signal will be for the student to clench every muscle in the body, and the other signal is to release all tension. The student will feel the difference in the body immediately, and the class will notice the difference in the sound.

2. Jana Iverson, Interview by author, Indiana University, August 1999.

Meet the Artist: CAROL VANESS

Soprano Carol Vaness's career encompasses regular appearances at the world's major opera houses and concert halls, an impressive catalog of recordings, and frequent television broadcasts in Europe and North America. Well known for her portrayals of the title role in Puccini's *Tosca* and Donna Anna in *Don Giovanni*, Ms. Vaness is drawn to arias that are not only "vocally beautiful, but . . . continue the action."[3]

When she prepares an aria, she begins by noting the tempo and dynamic markings: "Every punctuation can give the aria an intricate new meaning that can make the interpretation uniquely mine." Even though this act of analysis is essential to preparing an aria, Ms. Vaness cautions that one should never continue to analyze during a performance: "The performance is an expression of sound and emotion—through the words, to the audience."[4]

In addition to her own analysis, Ms. Vaness readily receives input from conductors, coaches, and directors: "Input is just that—input. A singer is responsible for the output." She suggests that singers remain open to the input of others but make it their own, "trying it on like a new dress and seeing which [interpretation] fits." Ms. Vaness encourages young singers to be "more of themselves . . . to look inside and find their unique gift."[5]

How important is the first note of the aria?

The opening measures before the singer sings the first note are crucial. Frequently the success of the audition will be achieved or not achieved in the first lines and notes of the aria. First, take time before you signal the accompanist to begin as a way to gather your thoughts, your energy, and your focus. An aria is a culmination of a powerful expression of emotion. Your energy is gathering, the expressive temperature is rising, and you have a need to sing! This dynamic change in emotional temperature to the place in which you must sing is very important. Otherwise the singer appears as if he or she is waiting to come in.

There are other spaces in the aria, sometimes only a rest. These "beats" of nonsinging space are opportunities for the singer to make choices that provide dramatic or musical clarity for the audience. When there are sudden changes of dynamics, tempo, key, and meter in the aria, we can also discover a dramatic connection for this musical change. Let us trust that the composer has made a change for a dramatic reason. Perhaps a decision has been made, the character has come to a dramatic conclusion, or there has been an emotional redirection. The singer-actor has many choices that come from the character, dramatic situation, or environment.

3. Carol Vaness, Interview by author, e-mail, 11 July 2001.
4. Ibid.
5. Ibid.

How can I use "creative play" to release tension in an aria?

Experimenting with the arias can be playful, freeing, and fun. It is important that these exercises are stripped from judgment or prejudices that come from universal conventions that suffocate creative work. One of the main points of these exercises is to demonstrate that unconventional choices can also "work" onstage.

Many of the exercises in this chapter encourage the singer to view an aria in a different way. One of the most interesting and productive ways to "play" with an aria is to use an arbitrary sampling of cards labeled with emotions (see Appendix A). The singer does not have an opportunity to rehearse these cards in advance, but if the performer does not resist and elects to let go, surprising results will be experienced by all (see Exercise 10.7).

If we rehearse too much and think too deeply, inhibitions can prevent us from going directly to the emotion we are seeking. When the class observes an emotional commitment, or an emotion that one would not generally associate with a particular aria and character, the result can be surprisingly powerful. It may not be a conventional reading of the aria, but all human expressions can be rich and textured, complex, and even contradictory. In each aria explore polar opposite emotions that are available to you through text, music, and characterization.

Even a traditional reading of an aria can be useful if labeled with specific emotions. When we first sing an aria, we often express many of the emotions in a very general way. By pairing an attitude with a specific section of an aria, we realize that the shades of emotion can be rich and varied. There is a world of difference between happy and ecstatic. The chart in Appendix A points out the number of choices available to us. Choice makes many of us uneasy and confused. On the other hand, choice can be powerful and freeing.

Exercises

11.1 PLAYING WITH LETTING GO

Objective: Releasing tension.

Directions: When the instructor holds up one arm, the body will tense while singing—every muscle will contract. Signaling with the other arm will indicate that the student should let go.

11.2 PLAYING WITH GESTURES AND MOVEMENT

Objective: Experimenting with movement and gesture.

Directions: Holding up one arm signals the request to be still with arms at the side. The other arm gives the singer permission to walk, move, pace, and gesture in any way without thinking about it.

11.3 PLAYING WITH THE FACE

Objective: Experimenting with expression.

Directions: One signal indicates that the singer should have a "poker face" with a blank stare. The other arm will ask for an active face in movement and mask.

11.4 MONOLOGUE/ARIA PROJECT

Objective: Exploring the text of an aria.

Directions: Each singer prepares an aria in English, but before it is sung, the singer puts the text into his or her own words, writes it all down, and presents it as a memorized monologue. The singer is in essence composing the music as he or she progresses, inventing the tempo and rhythm, the rests (spaces), the inflection, articulation, and dynamics. Without a dramatic tone, without "musical speech," the monologue will be flat and colorless. Once the singer brings the dramatic impulse to the words, the text has more meaning when sung.

11.5 THE SEARCH FOR DRAMATIC POLARITY

Objective: Examining opposite poles of a character during an aria.

Directions: Describe the opposing forces in a character during an aria. Clues to these opposites can be found in the character's background, the music and text in the aria, the context of the aria, and the environment. In many arias there is a struggle of some kind within the person. A decision needs to be made. The singer is working through the opposing forces.

Example: act 1 of *Manon*. The fifteen-year-old Manon is left alone in a courtyard while her cousin Lescaut has gone to get her luggage. It is her first journey away from home, and she is on her way to a convent on orders of her parents. Manon knows where she should stay to wait for her cousin, but she casts envious glances at actresses in their finery, representing a world that fascinates her. She can set up clear focus areas by predetermining where she should wait, where the actresses are standing in their finery that she envies, and from which direction Lescaut will enter. Manon is not polished or graceful, but naïve, innocent, confused, and full of unpredictable mood changes as she faces the "punishment" of being sent to the convent.

11.6 ARIA MAP PROJECT

Objective: Analyzing an aria.

Directions: Choose an aria in the original language to practice while keeping in mind several aspects of the performance (see list below). Notate them in the music, and then perform the aria for the class. I call this a notated "map" of an aria:

- Make a literal translation below the words of the original language.
- Choose focus areas for the environmental setting.
- Notate all focus shifts for intent.
- Make subtext notations.*
- Plan clear and specific emotions with focus shifts.

11.7 ARBITRARY EMOTION EXERCISE

Objective: Experimenting with interpretation of an aria.

Directions: The instructor holds up attitude cards (see Appendix A) that are arbitrarily chosen. The singer communicates each emotion while singing the aria.

11.8 ARIA WITHOUT THE VOICE

Objective: Analyzing movement during an aria using a video camera.

Directions: Use a video camera to record an aria presentation and play it back, turning the sound off. Look for seeing, focus, communicating, clear emotions, and gestures with meaning. Note any involuntary gestures or movement.

CONCLUSION

Arias are much more than merely a chance to display the voice. At best, they are a simple, direct, and clear message to the audience. The most powerful performances are ones that touch the hearts of the audience without artifice. Although a singer must practice an aria many times to feel secure and confident musically, some of the most exciting performances feel impromptu —as if the singer is experiencing the music for the first time.

Memorable performances are the ones that often bring something new to an aria. Although the quality and control of the singing voice is of utmost importance, it must still be thought of as a means to the end—the instrument that delivers the message of the music. It is up to the singer to determine how that message is received.

---

*The subtext is especially important in the spaces between phrases and the relationship between movement, emotion, and focus shifts (see Exercise 6.8).

CHECKLIST

- Determine to whom you are singing in each phrase. It can be a specific person, reflect a thought, or recount a memory or dream. Where is your focus?
- Write one of the attitudes from the chart (see Appendix A) under each phrase for emotional clarity.
- Write a literal subtext in your own words under each phrase so that it is clear that you understand each phrase of text in your own language.
- Record your aria with a video camera. Turn off the sound and write down specific emotions that are clear on your face.
- Describe in writing the environment. Close your eyes before you begin and describe the environmental elements in detail.

The Scene
Putting It All Together

12

INTRODUCTION

Scene study places the music and text, characterization, environment, and dramatic and musical analysis of the scene into the context of the whole opera. The discipline of scene study isolates each of these elements, or layers, and then integrates them into the whole.

In the workshop each layer can be peeled away and discussed or rehearsed separately through coaching of the music outside class, a discussion of the music with the scene participants and the class, or a musical presentation for the class before staging begins.

How should I study a scene?

Start by translating the text. If the text is in English and it is a translation, study the text in the original language as well. Often much is lost in translation. Do your research regarding the genesis of the composition overall, and the significance of when it was written in context of its stylistic period (see Appendix C).

Research is essential to understanding a scene. Determine exactly what the composer is giving to you dramatically. It is your job as you sing, interpret, move, and interact to give meaning to the work, to make it real. Some composers write a brief instrumental prelude (Mozart is a master at this) to paint the dramatic picture musically before you sing. Other composers (constrained by the period style) will present a B (middle) section that is an abrupt change in tempo and/or key, and therefore abrupt in mood as well. It is the singer's job to make a dramatic connection to the music, questioning the purpose of embellishments, cadenzas, rubati, sudden changes of dynamics, artic-ulations, and tessitura. With the aid of the director and conductor, we can decode the musical clues within a scene.

How can I bring the characters to life in a scene?

Find the parameters of the character in the scene you are preparing. The apparent contradictions can be challenging and interesting and ultimately give shape to the character. Other aspects for defining character are the physical at-tributes: station in life, age, and situation one is in. Unifying gestures can also tie together a character; they can be addressed when the singer begins to study a scene. Another element in character study is the relationship of the singer to the role. The singer is never able to inhabit the role completely. The singer's own personality is always incorporated. Look at the text that you are singing. How do *you* feel about the text and the music? What are the elements that you identify with, and what is foreign to you? Remember, portraying a role onstage is an interpretive art. It is creative rather than imitative and replicative.

Should I look at the scene in the context of the full opera?

Yes! Examine the scene by looking at it within the context of the entire work. What occurs before this scene and after? What exactly happens in this scene? Where are the dramatic "hot spots" where intense emotion is at its height? Exactly where are the "hinge points," or places where important deci-sions are made and dramatic changes occur? What do the characters want or need?

The environment, or atmosphere, of the opera is linked to the characters' dramatic situation in a scene. Images of the environment can come from the singer's imagination, directions in the score, production photos, videos, and reminiscences of live performance. It often helps to see how the sets, lights, and costumes are linked to the dramatic situation, characters, and music.

What is the best way to remember my staging?

The first step in staging the scene is for singers to learn the music and be able to put their scores down. Some singers prefer the initial blocking to be with book in hand so the singers can notate simple stage directions as they go along, especially when movements are specifically coordinated with music. In addition, some singers memorize more quickly if they know their blocking and the director's basic intentions, or reasons for movement.

However, many singers prefer to learn blocking and staging without the book in hand, notating later, so that "muscle memory" is utilized from the beginning. Opera singer Frederica von Stade will take the blocking directions from the director away from the rehearsal hall and practice them alone, making them her own.[1] Often after the initial blocking or staging, when the singers are completing the memorization process, the singing actor should go back to the score.

What clues to staging are already in the scene?

Singers can look for specific "directions" or clues in the music that provide dramatic clarity to each line of music, each facial expression and focus, and each movement. These clues come from musical dynamics, range, and articulation. Singers should continue to ask why the composer made specific choices. The specific answer is the choice the singing actor is making at the time.

For example, in act 1 of *Peter Grimes* by Benjamin Britten, Captain Balstrode, a retired merchant skipper, is questioning Peter Grimes in the hope that he will discover some uncovered truths about Grimes's past. An observant singer might note that Balstrode's first lines are broken by sudden piano dynamics. Is Balstrode concerned about other townspeople overhearing? Is he coming closer for the piano dynamic, speaking in confidence? The singer can guess at the composer's intent using the specific dramatic shading in the music.

Text is also of extreme importance. The inflection of important words says much about the character and their state of mind at each particular moment. In the same scene we learn a lot about Grimes because Balstrode is questioning him about why he lives the way he does. He comments about Grimes's reputation as an alleged murderer of an apprentice boy. A retired shipman, who must be a good judge of character to bring men on board, Balstrode has cross-examined countless men in his career. With the skill of a trial lawyer, Balstrode tries to get to the truth of the boy's death. This allows us to see Grimes open up for the first time, revealing a man who is at times both violent and poetic.

The environment is also crucial to this scene. Grimes is cleaning the nets on his boat, which is tied to the dock. His location is symbolic of his character. He is not out at sea, nor is he in the town. He is between the sea and land; he is adrift. Finally, the context of the scene is important. This scene takes place after a large crowd gathers. The forces of nature in the form of a gale cause the people to sing prayerfully, "Spare our coasts," as they scatter to their houses. While the exchange between Grimes and Balstrode occurs during a break in the weather, the specter of violent nature looms over the scene.

---

1. Frederica von Stade, Interview by author, e-mail, April 2000.

Should I approach a scene differently if it is in a foreign language?

Definitely. It is not enough for the singer to know what he or she is singing about; it is equally important for a singer to know what the other singers are saying. It affects the quality of listening and possible reactions to what is said. Nicholas Muni, Artistic Director of the Cincinnati Opera, begins staging work on each scene by having singers speak the text to each other using an English literal translation spoken in their own words. This helps the singers discover the meaning of exactly what is being said and how it is said before the blocking and music are added: "The actor must be fluent in the text—that is to say, well beyond the general meaning. For example, many key words have more than one translation meaning—I expect to see that the second, third, fourth listings from the dictionary have been considered."[2]

Should every movement onstage have meaning?

Ideally every movement onstage should be for a reason, but sometimes it seems that we are moving just to move. As a singer you must often bring your own meaning to a movement. While learning the notes and rhythms, blocking can be helpful when the "traffic patterns" are accompanied by knowing why the character crosses here or there. Sometimes the instructor or director provides this information early in the staging process, as well as environment specifics and focus areas. At other times, the singer must seek out the why and the intent of every motion on his or her own.

As singers learn and memorize the music, it is important to ask specific questions that relate to physicality, emotional state, and personal history. Verbalizing these answers before going onstage can help the singing actor to communicate clear thought processes. This clarity is perceived as energy by the audience—a vitality that comes from everyone onstage, whether a performer is singing or listening.

Should I get the opera workshop class involved in staging a scene?

I have always scheduled musical coachings and initial blockings outside of class time to save time and limit distraction. When the scenes are ready to be staged and put together, the singers come to class with the music and blockings memorized. They not only know where they are going—they know why. When we finally put legs on the scenes, the interaction of the class is extremely important for feedback, creative suggestions, and even support. If the

2. Nicholas Muni, Interview by author, Cincinnati, and e-mail, 8 February 2001.

atmosphere of the class is such that the colleagues will find the positive first and build on that, then confidence grows with the scene.

Choice is important in the creative process. Opera workshop can be your laboratory to explore many different possibilities, but in the final weeks before a public presentation, singers need continuity without interruption to discover the shape and meaning of the scene. To keep the class involved, I often ask them to take an important interactive role in rehearsal (see Exercises 12.4 and 12.5).

Exercises

12.1 IMPROVISATION IN REHEARSING A SCENE

Objective: Learning to paraphrase text.

Directions: Strip the text completely from the music to speak the lines of text in a scene without singing. In many cases this will involve paraphrasing and trying not to speak word for word. Paraphrasing is good because it involves thought processes in working through the lines and synthesizing thoughts. This can be a very useful exercise in working with the understanding of text and emotion as well as imagination and creative thought. It will take some practice to paraphrase your text for this exercise, but it can be rewarding. The singer's mind spends some time in understanding the text, interacting with other characters onstage, and going from the sustained time frame of music, with all of its constraints, to "real time." This is especially useful in rehearsing a recitative, which is closer to "real time."

12.2 PREPARING A SCENE IN THE ORIGINAL LANGUAGE

Objective: Paraphrasing your own English translation.

Directions: Preparing a scene in the original language takes more preparation to achieve its full value. All the words in the scene should be translated literally as well as paraphrased in such a way that makes sense in an ordered phrase. Singers sit and speak the text to each other with their own English translation of the text. This is a process that takes discussion and research and should take place before the staging.

12.3 STAGECRAFT AND THE SCENE

Objective: Rehearsing text without music to focus on dramatic conflict.

Directions: Begin by rehearsing the text without music in a spoken form to understand what the dramatic conflict is and the nature of the situation. For example, go back to the first act of Massenet's *Manon* when Des Grieux first meets Manon and falls in love. Manon is fifteen years old, youthfully impulsive, and on her way to the convent—never to be "free" again. If the two singers, Manon and Des Grieux, stand like wedding cake figures while singing and fall into a "safe" pose, the reality of the situation, stretched as it already is, is hopelessly lost. If we realize that Manon has very little time to decide, as her cousin Lescaut will arrive any minute, and that the environment of the scene is out in the open and during the day, not cloaked by night and without privacy, there is real urgency in their contact. This can be improvised in "real time," and then with music added.

A similar situation is in "La cí darem la mano," the duet between Don Giovanni and Zerlina in act 1 of *Don Giovanni*. Although the Don likes to take chances, there is also a sense of urgency for him to seduce Zerlina. Her intended Masetto and the others might show up any moment, and the scene takes place in an open square where someone may see them. The situation is urgent. In focusing on the characters of Zerlina and the Don, one notes a difference in class of which Don Giovanni is trying to take advantage. Traditionally, he is portrayed as smooth and suave, but with the sincerity of a used car salesman. Think of his ego. Remember the number of women he has conquered (the aria "Madamina, il catalogo è questo" sung by Leporello to Donna Elvira in act 1 catalogs them). At this stage of his career, do you think he will be patient throughout the entire duet? What might he say to "speed things along"? What might he do to show his impatience?

12.4 INTERACTIVE REHEARSAL

Objective: Involving the class in a scene staging.

Directions: As the class is watching a scene, ask for specific feedback. You can use some of the following strategies to build a positive environment:

- Use the Wesley Balk "Y" that means Yes (see Chapter 3). Students are asked to make the "Y" if they see energy. In a scene that is difficult to make real, I ask the class to give a "Y" as they see something that is real.[3]
- Designated students can work in tandem with singers to give signals of focus shift, facial expression, and release, followed by a "Y."
- Designated students can flash attitude cards to help singers define emotions for the audience.

12.5 INTERACTIVE REHEARSAL: TAKING NOTES

Objective: Involving the class in the process of staging.

Directions: The class is asked to take notes with specific goals in mind. De-

3. Wesley Balk, Institute residency, Minneapolis, 1989.

scribe the characteristics of a character and the emotional journey of the character in a scene. What happens to them during the journey?

12.6 TELLING A STORY AROUND A CAMPFIRE

Objective: Creating atmosphere with words and the face with descriptive language.

Directions: Using a scene from an opera, pretend you are telling a story around a campfire late at night. The class will sit around you as you tell the story, putting it within a context of environment and with a purpose of engaging your classmates' emotions.

CONCLUSION

Scene study is the analysis of the characters physically and emotionally in a particular scene. It is important to know what happens to these characters before and after the scene. What is the environment? The shape of the scene is important. What is the subtext? Where is the hinge (an important dramatic shift, a major decision, or an outside event that affects those in the scene)?

Beyond analysis, the synthesis of these elements is crucial to the interaction of the actors and to the development of the drama. Improvisation is often helpful. The use of attitude cards might build intensity and clarity of emotions. Playing with the scenes and the dramatic situation can be interesting and enlightening. Whatever the exercise, it should always seek to make the scene more real and immediate.

CHECKLIST

- Before the first rehearsal, understand the context of the scene in the opera.
    1. What is the importance of this particular scene?
    2. What is the shape of the scene musically and dramatically?
    3. What are the musical and dramatic "hinge points" of the scene?
    4. What are the conflicts in the scene?
    5. What do the characters need? How do they go about getting what they want?
- Investigate relationships, acting on impulses and reacting to impulses. Play with these by changing intents. How does this impact the scene?

The Opera
Preparing a Role

13

INTRODUCTION

Singing onstage is an art that is interactive in many different ways. Not only do we interact with others onstage, but we interact with coaches, stage directors, conductors, and of course the composer as well. This chapter presents several perspectives from those experts and artists who create and produce opera. We will hear from contemporary composers who work closely with singers during the rehearsal process. Stage directors will describe what a singer should "bring to the table" at the first staging rehearsal. Finally, conductors and coaches will outline their expectations for young singers at musical rehearsals.

THE COMPOSER'S POINT OF VIEW

Most opera composers of the past, including Mozart, Verdi, and Puccini, wrote for singers of the time and composed to their specific strengths. In the next section composers Mark Adamo, William Bolcom, Jake Heggie, and Kirke Mechem express their views on writing for the singer-actor today.

MARK ADAMO

Mark Adamo's adaptation of *Little Women* was commissioned by the Houston Grand Opera for the Houston Opera Studio, and its world premiere took place in Houston on 13 March 1998. Since then new productions have been mounted by the Kansas City Opera, Opera Pacific, Central City Opera,

Minnesota Opera, Indiana University Opera Theater, and the Glimmerglass Opera.

What do you look for as the singing actor rehearses your composition?

I want a singer excited by (and equipped to handle) the challenge of creating, with her body, a person from a document. It's not enough to read a phrase and accurately render the pitches and syllables. She needs the intuition, kinesthetic intelligence, and analytical skills to identify what the gesture is—the action, the intent that convinced the composer to finalize that phrase as the most precisely expressive of how that character's thinking sounds.

I want a singer bold enough to question received ideas of what correct or beautiful singing is. In *Little Women*, for example, I remember pitching the final line of an aria in the area of a singer's voice in which it lost a certain glamorous darkness and became hauntingly, plaintively brilliant. The timbral change was surprising and heartbreaking. But one singer, not unexpectedly, balked at first, because her training and taste urged her to maintain an even color throughout all her range   a useful, even elegant skill, but not crucial to the health of a voice, and a skill more apt to excite empty admiration than deep involvement in the theater.

What I'll offer a singer is enough knowledge of the way he or she works to vouchsafe that they can sing a role of mine healthily throughout a long run. In return, I need them to enter my world with as much eagerness to learn a new style—which is a way of hearing as much as a way of singing—as they would when learning, say, Britten after Strauss, or Verdi after Purcell.

What advice would you give singers as they prepare a new opera role?

Start from the greatest question—What is this opera about? Then locate the overarching goal of your character within that design. Assume, then, that every choice in the score—verbal, intervallic, registral, rhythmic, dynamic, orchestrational—was made to express that goal, and try to identify and then embody those choices. Not only why is this phrase marked piano, but why does this piano phrase succeed the previous *mezzo forte*? Why is this word pitched on low A?

In making a piece, I try to compose it from the point of view of every participant—singer, actor, conductor, director, designer, player. A singer investigating a role in my own work will thus find, so to speak, a thousand roads to Rome. For example, I once informed a singer that the music her duet partner was singing in act 2 was based closely on her own quite different-sounding music from an earlier scene. Now, the scene was written so that you didn't need to know this detail to make sense of it: the words, the actual aural character of the new music conveyed the main narrative point. But this small point empowered her to apply yet another band of her intelligence. She wasn't confined just to her talents for interpreting text or exploiting her vocal colors or using dynamic changes to make points. As long as you're singing a role—even (especially!) during performance—assume there are new things to find. A "finished" performance is just that.[1]

WILLIAM BOLCOM

Dr. Bolcom received the Pulitzer Prize for music in 1988 and has received commissions from numerous opera companies, including the Chicago Lyric Opera. He most recently has composed and premiered the operas *A View from the Bridge* (1999) and *McTeague* (1992), both at Lyric Opera.

What are the trends in opera today?

Our growing American operatic tradition will, by most accounts, be wordier but also more theatrically congruent than, say, middle Verdi could get away with. Diction can only convince an audience if the singer understands the text profoundly; otherwise there is no chance to communicate fully.[2]

JAKE HEGGIE

The music of Jake Heggie is being performed internationally and recorded by such noted singers as sopranos Renée Fleming, Sylvia McNair, Dawn Upshaw, and Carol Vaness; mezzo-sopranos Frederica von Stade, Susan Graham, and Jennifer Larmore; countertenor Brian Asawa; and baritone Thomas Hampson. A winner in the 1995 Schirmer National Art Song Competition and the composer of over 130 songs as well as solo instrumental, chamber, choral, and orchestral works, Heggie has received commissions from symphony orchestras and opera companies across America. His most recent opera success, *Dead Man Walking*, was commissioned by the San Francisco Opera for their 2000 season.

What skills do young singers need today?

Great singer-actors are first, and foremost, interested in the *connection* of the words and music, and how best to communicate the story to another

1. Mark Adamo, Interview by author, e-mail, 3 January 2001.
2. William Bolcom, Interview by author, e-mail, 12 January 2001.

human being. They put themselves completely into the song; they know every turn of every phrase. They have listened carefully to hear how the composer has responded to each phrase, how he has colored every word. If the song mentions leaves falling off of trees, for example, the intelligent singer will want to know what color the leaves are; why are they falling off the tree; what season is it; where am I; in what part of the world; am I alone; is this a good thing; is it a tragedy; am I filled with resignation or joy? All of that.

I think every good singer does exactly what the composer does—starts with the text, understands it, and then works on inhabiting it convincingly. Phrasing, breathing, coloring—all of these come from understanding the text and how the composer has set it. I think many singers forget, too, that the notes on the page are a road map only. I always take as an example the great jazz singers, like Ella Fitzgerald. Look at the music and then listen to what she does with it—amazing. Classical singers can learn a lot from that. Obviously there isn't as much freedom as in a jazz song, but it's not too far off. The text, the phrasing—they all lead a singer to push and pull a little bit here and there to *tell the story*.

What is missing in some performances?

I think one thing that is missing in many singers' performances is the sense of motivation and purpose. It is so important that a singer feels he or she has a reason to sing what they are singing, and that it be sung rather than spoken. I've heard so many singers perform and wondered, "Now why did they pick that to sing? Why did he or she need to sing that?" Again, this has to do with feeling connected to the music.

One thing I think that has been greatly overlooked with voice recitals is the necessity for a director—unless the singer possesses uncommonly good instincts, and even then it's not a bad idea. A recital is a theatrical event, and every aspect needs to be treated as such. Simple gestures, or the lack of them, should be thought out in advance to enhance the whole experience for the singer and the listener. A cabaret singer would never think of doing a full evening without a director, and yet classical singers do it all the time.

The focus of singing and performing is to tell a story—to share a journey—and I think singers often get so wrapped up in the technical part of it that the communication becomes secondary. This is backwards. The technique is only a means to an end, not an end in and of itself.[3]

3. Jake Heggie, Interview by author, e-mail, 27 December 2000.

KIRKE MECHEM

Kirke Mechem is the composer of over two hundred published works in almost every musical form. His three-act opera *Tartuffe* has had nearly 250 performances since its premiere by the San Francisco Opera in 1980. One of the most popular contemporary operas, it has been presented in Mandarin in China and translated into German, Japanese, and Russian. It is currently being translated into Czech for the National Theater in Prague.

What do you look for in a young singer?

Young singing actors today should possess flexible voices, command of language and diction, plus an intelligence, musicianship, and superb acting ability that opera did not demand fifty years ago. The singer who gets the job today (many have the voice) is the one who learns fast and acts convincingly.

Singers should have the ability to sing English with such good diction that nearly every word can be understood. It *can* be done, but it takes work and a lot of practice. In a comic opera like *Tartuffe* (and many other American operas), supertitles should not be necessary in a small hall before an American audience.

How should a singer prepare a role for one of your operas?

Start with the character. This means reading the entire libretto first. Without knowing the character inside and out and how he or she relates to everyone else, you are just singing in the dark. Every phrase should convey by the tone of voice (just as we do when speaking) how the character feels about what is being said. Is he or she angry, happy, teasing, deceptive, afraid, or unsure?[4]

THE STAGE DIRECTOR'S POINT OF VIEW

What should the singer "bring to the table" at the first staging rehearsal? In this section stage directors Tito Capobianco, Matthew Lata, Joshua Major, and Nicholas Muni describe what they look for in established professionals and young artists alike.

TITO CAPOBIANCO

Born in Buenos Aires, Argentina, Tito Capobianco is one of the leading opera directors and producers of his generation. He has directed at all of the major opera centers in the world and has served as General and Artistic Direc-

4. Kirke Mechem, Interview by author, e-mail, 19 December 2000.

tor of the New York City Opera, San Diego Opera, and Pittsburgh Opera. Also known for his work with young singers, Mr. Capobianco created the Juilliard Opera Center and the Pittsburgh Young Artist Program and has taught at the Academy of Vocal Arts, Music Academy of the West, Yale University, and Indiana University.

What should a singer bring to the first staging rehearsals?

Humility. This comes from the singer studying the role inside out: knowing the music, the libretto word for word—including what the other singers are singing about—the history, and the style. When the singer has undertaken this intense preparation, humility is the result. Another discipline that the young singer should bring to the first staging rehearsal is a thorough thinking through of his or her character. I personally observed this at Indiana University before the first staging of *Rigoletto,* when Mr. Capobianco, without warning, asked pointed questions about the background of each student's character. No aspect was deemed unimportant, as Mr. Capobianco expected the students to have thought about their characters in great detail.[5]

MATTHEW LATA

Matthew Lata has directed operas from *Aïda* to *Die Zauberflöte* with opera companies from Anchorage to Tulsa. He has directed at the Lyric Opera Center for American Artists in Chicago and has taught at the University of Missouri in Kansas City, Yale University, and Northwestern University. He will direct *Die Zauberflöte* at the Chicago Lyric Opera in 2002.

What are your expectations for the first staging rehearsal?

In a perfect world a singer comes to rehearsal fully prepared. This means, first of all, knowing not only notes, but knowing the meaning of every word to be sung. It also means knowing the meaning of everything that is said while you are onstage. General ideas or singing translations are not enough. Look up every word, or find someone who can help. This is tedious, but you have to do it only once. To present a scene naturally, a singer should be able to function within a scene as if it were performed in their own language.

How should a singer prepare a role?

A singer's preparation should include not only learning notes and music but also developing a point of view about your character. This means, first of

5. Tito Capobianco, Interview by author, Indiana University residency, February 2001.

all, knowing the entire piece and how your character functions within it. It means having an informed knowledge of the character and how the world looks through that character's eyes. It means knowing something about the history of the piece and, perhaps, why it was written the way it was written. It means having a sense of the period in which it was written, even if the production is not set in that period.

This does not mean locking yourself into decisions that make you inflexible. Quite the contrary. It means being able to react to ideas from conductors and directors without losing your identity in the process. The best productions—and certainly the most rewarding experiences—are often the result of collaborations, not a series of dictations from conductor and director to the singer.

Do not automatically assume, though, that you will get a lot of help. If you are called upon to step into a production on short notice or are second or third cast somewhere, you may get little or no rehearsal. They are not necessarily hiring you to sing Mimi. They are hiring your Mimi. Your characterization should be flexible and complete enough to function in any production. You should be able to perform the character both independently and as the result of a rehearsal process. In the end, you are the person who must deliver the goods onstage in front of the audience.[6]

JOSHUA MAJOR

Joshua Major has directed more than eighty productions throughout North America. He is a regular guest at Yale University and is on the faculty at the University of Michigan. During the summer he is a stage director at the Israel Vocal Arts Institute.

How should singers prepare for the first staging rehearsal?

I expect and prefer singers to show up having thought about what they are singing. That they consider the content and meaning of what they are singing is vital. I am interested in meaning and purpose. That they understand why they are expressing something is vital. I am not particularly interested in lengthy character descriptions; rather, I am interested in why a character is expressing a particular point of view. In the end I am interested in what the singer is doing when they are onstage. Feelings are vital, but I am not a director who directs through the dictation of what a person is supposed to feel. When the singer shows up and describes all the emotions they need to feel I get worried. I am more interested in the doing.[7]

6. Matthew Lata, Interview by author, e-mail, 11 December 2000.
7. Joshua Major, Interview by author, e-mail, 8 January 2001.

NICHOLAS MUNI

Nicholas Muni, Artistic Director of Cincinnati Opera, has directed nearly two hundred productions with some of the finest opera companies in North America, Europe, and Australia. From 1988 to 1993 he served as Artistic Director of Tulsa Opera, where he produced and directed two American premieres: Verdi's *Le Trouvère* (the French version of *Il Trovatore*) and Rossini's *Armida*. Both premieres were broadcast on National Public Radio's "World of Opera" series. His most recent world premiere was Michael Daugherty's opera *Jackie O*, based on the life of Jaqueline Kennedy Onassis, with the Houston Grand Opera and Banff Center for the Arts.

What are your expectations for the first staging rehearsals?

First staging rehearsal expectations: music memorized, text translated, ability to paraphrase text, thoughts on the character within a flexible mental framework. There are expectations in character preparations. If it is an historical character, I expect that a fair amount of research and reading was done about the person and/or historical events surrounding the situation upon which the opera is based. For example, for *Tosca* I would expect basic knowledge of Bonaparte's imperialistic activities. For any opera based on a play or novel, I would expect that the actor has read the original source material.

What are the important steps in preparing a role?

Knowing the literal meaning of each word of the text. Melding music to text—textual stress and inflection in relationship to rhythm, pitch, phrase markings, and dynamic markings. Knowing the super-objective for the character. Knowing the historical background information, if any. Giving thought to the character background (personal history and circumstances—Tosca grew up as a shepherdess, for example). Reading up on the circumstances surrounding the composition of the piece—what was going on in the composer's life at the time? Why did he or she write the opera? Are there any political circumstances that might be pertinent?[8]

THE CONDUCTOR'S AND COACH'S POINTS OF VIEW

Conductors and coaches work with singers before the first staging rehearsals. First, coaches assist singers in learning notes and rhythms, handling any vocal "rough spots." Then conductors work with individuals and ensembles

8. Nicholas Muni, Interview by author, e-mail, 8 February 2001.

to help the singer communicate musically. In this section conductors Julius Rudel and Patrick Summers and coaches Martin Katz and John Wustman describe their expectations for musical rehearsals.

JULIUS RUDEL

Born in Vienna, Julius Rudel was the Musical Director of New York City Opera from 1957–79, developing the company into one of the most enterprising in the United States. He is best known for his work with singer Beverly Sills as a conductor and mentor. Highly regarded for his creativity and professionalism, Mr. Rudel has received numerous awards.

Mr. Rudel is known as a consummate musician who has worked with some of the greatest singers. I recently discovered how passionate he is about the stage: he frequently attends theater productions, and when speaking with him after he observed an Indiana University Opera Theater production, I found his comments very interesting. Yes, he spoke of the voices and the orchestra, but it seemed as if much of his focus was on what was happening onstage and the choices the singers were making as singing actors.

How should singers prepare for a music rehearsal?

I expect all singers to be well prepared musically, but I do not want the cast members to be blank slates. They should have ideas about the musical/dramatic connections that they can work with.[9]

PATRICK SUMMERS

Currently Patrick Summers is the Music Director of the Houston Grand Opera and Principal Guest Conductor of the San Francisco Opera.

What are your expectations at a musical rehearsal?

Arm yourself with as much knowledge as you can—then throw out all the knowledge and let your imagination take over. I am continually inspired by the imagination of gifted singers.[10]

MARTIN KATZ

Martin Katz is one of the preeminent accompanists and coaches today. He has collaborated with most of the great stars of the opera world, including Frederica von Stade, Kiri Te Kanawa, Cecilia Bartoli, José Carreras, Evelyn

9. Julius Rudel, Interview by author, telephone, 21 February 2001.
10. Patrick Summers, Interview by telephone and letter, 17 January 2001.

Lear, Thomas Stewart, and David Daniels. He has collaborated with Marilyn Horne for more than thirty years.

What are your expectations for a singer when they walk in your studio?

The text should be translated. In tonal music I rarely have to teach notes. Of course, there always is the odd unlearned pitch or rhythm to be corrected, but I'm speaking generally. In atonal music (*Wozzeck, Moses und Aaron,* even some Richard Strauss) I don't agree to coach a role unless I know I have time to deal with pitches myself. If I can't figure out how to find them, I have no method for helping my customer. Finally, knowledge of the story of the opera, who the singer's character is, who the people around him or her are or were.[11]

JOHN WUSTMAN

John Wustman began his career as accompanist for the Robert Shaw Chorale and has performed regularly in the world's musical capitals with Elisabeth Schwarzkopf, Birgit Nilsson, Régine Crespin, Renata Scotto, Christa Ludwig, Roberta Peters, Mirella Freni, Carlo Bergonzi, and Nicolai Gedda. Professor Wustman has appeared frequently as accompanist with Luciano Pavarotti, including the historic recitals at the Metropolitan Opera House and a series of master classes broadcast nationally by PBS.

How prepared should a singer be before a coaching?

The singer should have translated the foreign language as carefully and as literally as possible. Understanding of each word is vital. A general overall translation is not sufficient. What I do is to help students with the understanding of the text and music.[12]

CONCLUSION

Whether it is the person who created the opera, or the person who brings that opera to life, the professionals in power expect singers to be prepared. But as the interviews in this chapter reveal, "prepared" can mean different things to different people. The composer expects singers to understand the intent of the opera and the emotions of the character. The stage director insists that the singer should know the meaning of "every word" and has thought about the characterization. Conductors and coaches stress that the singer is a creative collaborator. In each case the singer is asked to look deeply and intelligently into their role, while staying flexible and open to inspiration and the suggestions of others.

11. Martin Katz, Interview by author, e-mail, 1 January 2001.
12. John Wustman, Interview by author, e-mail, 27 January 2001.

Performance Anxiety
Facing Fear

14

INTRODUCTION

Performance anxiety is a natural part of every performance. The problem occurs when anxiety limits our performance. If this happens, we can fall into a dangerous pattern of behavior that may be repeated in every performance. At this point we must change our behavior, which is not always easy to do.

It takes an expert to guide us on this journey. Stephen D. Curtis teaches a course on applied performance psychology at Indiana University. In it he instructs musicians and athletes about the physiology and anatomy of anxiety as well as its consequences for mental and behavioral impairment. This course examines what is known about anxiety and how it affects the body and brain, and it introduces students to techniques that are effective in controlling and eliminating anxiety. Dr. Curtis also teaches students about the internal psychodynamics that determine an individual's level of achievement as well as those factors that seem to be important for creating very high, or "Zone," levels of performance.

In the following interview Dr. Curtis answers some of the most commonly asked questions about performance anxiety and shares some of his favorite exercises to relieve that anxiety.

What is the definition of performance anxiety?

Performance anxiety is the fear that many performers experience before and during performances. Psychologists see performance anxiety as a special case of a broader fear called *social anxiety,* or fear of people.

It is also a major determiner of success in the music industry. Many performers with substantial talent fail to continue careers in music because of the discomfort and/or debilitating consequences of unchecked performance anxiety. Alternatively, other performers with lesser talent but freedom from performance anxiety can prosper.

Why is performance anxiety so debilitating?

Performance anxiety is a generalized fear that distorts thinking and perception as well as the performer's ability to move physically. All functions of the brain and body are disturbed by performance anxiety, and the performer is incapable of performing at a high level.

Of particular concern for musicians is the finding that fear causes subjects in hearing tests to be unable to make fine distinctions in pitch: that is, a fearful musician can be playing or singing off-key and not be aware of it. It is also true that the subtleties of muscular coordination required to sing or play are diminished with fear.

What causes performance anxiety?

Performance anxiety occurs because of thoughts and learned responses to performance situations. The most important psychological contributor to the onset of performance anxiety is a performer's concern for, or fear of, the outcome of the performance: that is, the performer's thoughts become focused on an imagined negative outcome or failure. Even though this thought pattern concerns the future, that is, the end of the performance, the fear that accompanies an imagined failure occurs in the present tense, either before or during a performance.

Performance anxiety can increase rapidly within a performance as the initial fear causes the impairments in performance described above and errors in performance occur. After occurring a number of times, the fear response can become a conditioned or learned response to performance situations. As the response becomes more firmly conditioned with repetitions, it becomes harder to control or "unlearn."

What can be done to combat performance anxiety?

Frequently I hear sports and performance psychologists and teachers state that performers "must simply learn to play with nerves." I disagree with this and believe that a performer suffers with performance anxiety because he or she has failed to develop the mental and emotional strength that will allow more positive thoughts and feelings.

Thoughts become stronger and more available as they are practiced repeatedly. For many performers, the thoughts and emotions that accompany performance anxiety are extremely well practiced. Years of "simply playing with nerves" have created very strong habits, and performances *must* be fear-provoking. These performers are very good at being afraid. Others have "nerves" only occasionally and are always concerned that they might "show up" and ruin a performance.

In all cases the only effective strategy for consistently controlling performance anxiety is for a performer to develop and maintain significant mental strength in his or her ability to create nonfearful thoughts and emotions. This mental ability can be practiced and maintained through repetition. Just as the performance of a piece of music becomes stronger with practice, so too does a person's mental ability to think calming, relaxing, and reassuring thoughts.

I have created a sequence of mental exercises that allow these skills to be developed. They require the use of a tape recorder and consist of a progressive relaxation sequence, confident self-statements, and visualizations of successful performance. [See Dr. Curtis's Web site, www.beaconsystems1.ypgs.net, for more information.]

How can I relax onstage?

Relaxing onstage is again a mental skill that can be learned and practiced. I believe that the most debilitating component of any performer's fear response is the hypoxia or low blood oxygen that results from an inadequate breathing pattern. Fear-induced muscle tension in the chest serves to restrict inhalations, and an increased rate of respirations can result in rapid upper chest breathing that does not allow for adequate oxygen exchange in the lungs. Feelings of panic simply because of low oxygen can dramatically increase performance anxiety, and the mental and physical impairments due to low oxygen can result in confusion, uncoordinated movements, or even "blanking out," which is where a well-known score is completely "forgotten."

To combat this, I encourage my students to learn and practice slow, deep chest or diaphragmatic breathing, counting their exhalations [see Exercise 14.2]. This technique can rapidly increase blood oxygen levels, and a feeling of well-being and relief can be experienced. The upper layers of the cerebral cortex of the brain are the most sensitive tissues in the body to a lack of oxygen, but they are also responsible for the sensation of hearing and the initiation of movement. Increased blood oxygenation can rapidly reverse the ill effects of hypoxia.

Another very effective strategy is to focus fully on the present tense, that is, the music that is currently happening [see Exercise 14.1]. Full immersion in the present tense with a focus on sensory awareness can effectively block the damaging distraction of thoughts about outcomes in the future, or mistakes from the past.

What do you believe is the most important psychological factor affecting the success of a performer?

I believe that the self esteem of a performer ultimately determines the life quality that he or she will create. This means that performers with high self-esteem will, by all means possible, create success because they fully believe that they deserve it. Low self-esteem creates an expectation for failure, and individuals with low self-esteem can be very creative in sabotaging even great natural talent.

What can a performer do to improve self-esteem?

Again, I believe that hard work can create changes in the thinking patterns that make up self-esteem. Specifically, I define self-esteem as the tone of a person's self-judgments. Low self-esteem is characterized by critical, harsh, and negative self-judgments. High self-esteem is typified by accepting and positive self-judgments. Every performer can create with sustained and repetitive practice a more positive pattern of self-talk and self-judgment, and it is, I believe, a necessary prerequisite for significantly improved levels of performance.

It can sound trite to an uninformed ear to say that one's self-talk determines one's success, but I have found it to be the most important predictor of success, in many cases eclipsing skill level and even natural ability. A performer can have both skill and innate natural talent, but if he or she does not believe that he or she is deserving of success, success will not come and stay. The person who feels unworthy of success will find a multitude of ways to sabotage any possibility of sustaining a pattern of success. Frequently, I think, unaddressed performance anxiety itself is an out that performers with low self-esteem will use to sabotage or end a promising career.

I also have found that a performer's musical skills improve after self-esteem increases because the expectation of greater success provides the motivation for more, and more effective, musical practice. I will always predict that if one fully believes that one is deserving of success, then success—to the limits of one's natural abilities—*will* occur.

I encourage my students to work on confirming and improving self-esteem multiple times each day using a tape recorder. I believe that new thoughts are learned best in a condition of relaxation, so I always encourage a progressive relaxation sequence prior to positive self-statements. [See Dr. Curtis's Web site for more information.]

How can a performer find the "Zone"?

My guess is that to be very successful as a musician, one must "be in the Zone" fairly frequently. Audiences are enraptured by Zone performances, and it seems clear that human beings are drawn to those who can display this amazing ease of performance.

I believe that the Zone occurs when certain slow brain wave patterns are created during a performance. These electroencephalogram patterns known as alpha and theta are typically only observed in subjects who are immobile and have their eyes closed, but during these relatively rare Zone occasions these patterns are apparently happening despite the mobility and vision of the performer. In these Zone performances, very high levels of creativity and musicianship are accompanied by significant feelings of calm, confidence, and ease. The musician is fully engaged in the moment with no concern for the future, that is, the outcome.

I believe that the Zone will occur for skilled musicians occasionally and unpredictably. I do believe, however, that there are a variety of lifestyle issues that can allow a person to live day to day with generally slower brain wave patterns, patterns that are closer to the Zone. Living closer to the Zone makes its occurrence more likely. These lifestyle issues read like a stress management, healthy living manual. Positive changes include eliminating caffeine and other chemical stimulants, improving exercise, diet, and sleep patterns, as well as managing the stressors of life more effectively. When a performer can approach a performance with a sense of true calm and confidence—fearlessly—then a Zone performance is possible.

The bottom line on creating the Zone is this: If a performer can live close to the Zone off the stage, the Zone is more likely to occur when on the stage. All of life is reflected in a performer's art, and the best art comes from those who live the best lives.

Exercises

14.1 REALITY CHECK

Objective: Disrupting the pattern of "numbing" and fixating on the distracting past or future. In moments of anxiety the field of vision narrows, and our senses shut down for defense.

Directions: Become keenly aware of the present moment. Look at your environment and examine objects with thought and interest. Be aware of sights, smells, and sounds. The patterns of the past often repeat memories of past auditions or performances. Future fixations can be thoughts of placing oneself out of "danger" and into the safety of completing the audition or performance. Other future thoughts or distractions focus on the "prize" rather than the present moment. Take a deep breath, and stay in the moment.

14.2 DEEP BREATHING

Objective: Bringing more oxygen into the body. Rapid, shallow breath causes hyperventilation.

Directions: Open the throat and release the body. Keep the knees released and the spine stretched. The arms should feel heavy. Take a cleansing breath, breathing deeply through the nose with the mouth closed. Exhale through the mouth, feeling tension leave the body with each breath.

14.3 ZZZ BREATHING

Objective: Feeling the body "under the breath" with the support of the "zzz."

Directions: Breathe deeply, and make a "zzz" sound with the mouth and lips as you breathe out. Keep breathing while making the sound "zzz." When the body is free, you should feel the torso "underneath the hum."

14.4 THE AHHH BREATH

Objective: Combining the deep breath (Exercise 14.2) with the calming "ahhh."

Directions: Breathe deeply, open the throat, and whisper "ahhh" through the throat as you exhale. This is a calming exercise and a warm-up before speaking or singing.

14.5 MENTAL REHEARSAL

Objective: Using visualization to create a positive performing environment.

Directions: Close your eyes and visualize the performance setting. Picture yourself walking onstage, taking control of the stage, and starting the performance. Each time you feel tension or your breathing becomes shallow, take a deep breath (Exercise 14.2) and release the tension. Stay in the moment (Exercise 14.1) and visualize success.

If you have a chance to go onstage before the performance, walk through the staging, speak the text, and sing key musical phrases. Each time you feel anxiety, dip into the positive memories that come from your mental rehearsal. During the performance, take control. Do not signal the pianist to begin until you are ready. Because you have already done this successfully in your mind, you can approach the performance with a sense of calm and confidence.

CONCLUSION

Performance anxiety is not just in your mind—it is in your body. It is a natural physical response to stress. Your daily habits can help or hinder the management of performance anxiety. A mental toughness is required to change patterns of behavior. For example, too much sugar and caffeine may hinder concentration. The ability to find mental and physical rest is crucial. Exercise is helpful for physical and mental health. Yoga and t'ai chi exercises can release tension and sharpen focus. Remember that your instrument is not just the larynx; it is the entire body.

Those who display performance anxiety patterns often begin to think of past experiences, or their thoughts drift to the future and outcomes. In the midst of a performance, they might ponder, "What will happen if . . . ?" The best way to change this pattern is to stay in the moment, not to worry about the high note to come. Engage yourself in each phrase and each moment. Realize that when you are afraid it is because you have made a conscious decision to be afraid. You have the decisive control in this matter.

We can set up a blueprint for success when planning for a performance without anxiety. This mental and physical plan puts the singer in control of the situation. By learning about this natural physical reaction to stress, we can control it, and in so doing take control of our performance.

CHECKLIST

- Establish a food routine that gives you fuel but is not hard to digest.
- Establish a physical warm-up routine that gets the blood moving in the body.
- Be extremely well prepared in your memorization and technique.
- Establish a comfortable vocal warm-up that does not tire your voice.
- Take control of the performance when singing an audition or in a competition.
- Mentally rehearse the performance, running through it in your mind.
- Walk through the staging; speak the text and sing key musical phrases.
- When possible before a performance, walk through the set to feel more "at home" and comfortable.

Careers in Opera
Stepping Out

15

INTRODUCTION

This chapter is an overview of the research and steps necessary to begin laying the foundation of a career for the young singer. It is never too early to begin to investigate what it takes to have a career in this field. After all, if you are serious about studying to become a professional singer-actor, it is important to know what this life is about, and how young singers begin building their careers. That being said, I have found that those who have attained a career in opera each has a unique story to tell about his or her own personal journey. Although the path is different, there are elements in common that we can draw on to help show us the way. This overview will discuss these elements as well as guide you to materials to help you in your own journey.

What should the young singer do first?

If you are studying to be a professional singer, find out all you can now about the field. Acquaint yourself with the important operas in the repertoire, and identify those works that have roles you would like to sing someday. Learn about the important singers in opera and determine what sets them apart and makes them special to the public. Opera on television and video is one way to acquaint yourself with the repertoire, but it is no substitute for live opera.

If you live near a regional opera company, see if you can become involved as a volunteer in any aspect of production, backstage as well as onstage. Eager young singers are needed in every regional opera chorus, and it is an excellent way to learn the repertoire as well as observe and meet those singers who have maintained a professional career. Endeavor to keep in contact with the professional singers you have met as well as all musical and production staff.

How can I find out about new opportunities?

The opera world is a very small one, and networking is crucial for information as well as support. Don't forget your fellow students. They can provide an important network of support. Frequently auditions and opportunities will come by word of mouth, and the student singer must be open to every bit of information. Keep your eye on bulletin boards. Read the local newspaper. Sometimes information will be incomplete or filtered, but the young singer must always have his or her ear to the ground.

Start early to investigate professional opportunities through research. If possible, young singers should join Opera America (www.operaam.org). This national organization offers information about the careers of aspiring singers in specific singer guides. Their bulletins provide notices about auditions for young singer programs and competitions, telling you how to apply and audition, details of each program, and deadlines for submitting applications. Keep a written record of all contacts, and investigate all professional leads. Take on a businesslike and thorough manner in the process, and your organization will pay off.

What if I am only an undergraduate student?

Even before your voice has the maturity to sing a major role, there are a number of proactive steps to take in preparing yourself for a career in professional singing. First, make sure you are providing yourself with a solid vocal technique. It will be your foundation as a singer. For one reason or another, there will be many times that you will not feel in tip-top shape physically onstage. The solid technique you developed in college will be there for you. Learning to sing is the technical craft of finding out how to develop range, agility, and the dynamics needed to express many emotions.

Another aspect of the craft is musicianship. It is crucial in your relationship with one of the most powerful members of the production team—the conductor. Conductors can propel a young singer to high professional levels when they respect their musicianship and enjoy working with them as a musical colleague. This is the time to build your reading skills and musicianship. Work on your languages, not only in the sense of diction, but also in comprehension. If you can attend a summer institute or spend a semester abroad, it is all the better for applying your knowledge and acquiring conversational language skills you may not learn in the classroom. It may serve you best to first concentrate on one language. If you like the idea of working in Europe as a singer, German will be your best choice for a language to start learning now because many of the opera houses with opportunities for young singers are in German-speaking countries.

Although you may presently be studying in a conservatory of music which allows you to study predominantly musical subjects, make sure that you receive a well-rounded education. Literature, writing, history, and the visual arts are all-important educational applications to the singing career. Now is the time to realize that although there is a craft to be learned in becoming a professional singer, you should think of yourself as an artist first. This involves acquiring excellent communication and research skills.

What should I do once I get to graduate school?

Graduate school should be an opportunity for you to begin to perform roles. You will want to choose a school in which you will find a teacher who will guide you in this endeavor. For many graduate students, this means finding a teacher of your own vocal type who has sung several of the roles you would eventually like to perform. The voice teacher will be your most important constant during graduate school, so the chemistry in this working relationship is crucial.

This is a time in which networking becomes more important, and you will see your fellow students auditioning and entering competitions as their voices mature and they gain more experience. It is crucial at this stage for the young singer to be patient and soak up as much knowledge as possible before auditions begin. It is a time to learn as much as possible about your own voice and goals.

How can I get ready for an audition?

There is no denying the fact that the audition process will be your means for advancing into young artist programs and a career. Most singers recognize that the audition is markedly different from the experience of public performance. Auditioning is a skill, and learning to audition well is a critical factor in a singing career. There are a number of factors beyond our control in the audition process. We don't always know what the auditioner will want us to sing, though the first choice is usually ours. We don't know what the auditioner is specifically looking for vocally or dramatically. Since tastes vary from person to person, we must realize that we are not going to please everyone, and trying to please everyone is futile. However, a few factors are within our control.

First, be fully prepared. Present music with which you are very familiar. Do not use the audition to break in a new piece you have never sung in front of anyone. Sing your arias for anyone and everyone who will hear them. If the piece is a struggle for you, and you have to have a very good day to be able to do it well, reconsider the choice. If the aria requires agility, trills, or other decorative figures, make sure that you have these within your grasp and do them well without undue concentration that diverts your focus away from your performance. The rule of thumb is to sing an aria you sing well *now* rather than an aria that you may someday sing well.

In an audition you will usually have the opportunity to choose your opening piece. Your choice should be a piece that you could "roll out of bed" and sing. In other words, you could sing it well no matter how you are feeling. Try to pick a piece that you particularly love to sing, for this shows to good effect in an audition. Wear clothes that feel comfortable but are not too casual. It appears that men no longer need to wear a formal suit to audition but may opt for a turtleneck and sports coat or even an open collar if desired. The audition is not the place to wear a new pair of shoes for the first time, especially if they are unsteady or slick. It is good not to be too flamboyant or flashy in dress— nothing that would distract from the performance. If you are auditioning for a particular role, you may consider hinting at your character subtly in dress. Consider a shawl for an older female character, a jacket that is more formal for an aristocratic character, or a simple shirt for a servant.

Make sure you include an introduction in your practice. Rehearse saying, "Hello, my name is _____, and I would like to sing _____." Try your introduction a number of different ways. It should be friendly, businesslike without being stiff, not too casual or too slow. Those auditioning you will watch you from your entrance until you leave the stage. You will even be judged by how you greet and interact with the pianist. Rather than be concerned and anxious about it, look at this as an opportunity to show yourself to them as a person that they will want to have in their program or company. The only way to know how to do it is to practice with others. Put yourself in the chair of those who listen to the audition to know what it is like to be in the "other" place.

Some auditions for young artist programs include an informal interview after you sing. This is an important part of the audition, as it presents your "real" personality. They want to know what you are like as a person, what you might be like to work with, and whether or not you will fit into their program. Again, it is important to speak naturally but clearly, friendly but not cloying. It is annoying to work with someone who is overly anxious to please. Be honest and straightforward, not just saying what you think will impress them. Above all, singers should be confident but not arrogant.

Singers who audition frequently tell me of routines that border on the superstitious. One of my students will eat an apple before the audition. A routine can be comforting and reassuring as long as it doesn't become compulsive. Try a number of routines that include warming up the body as well as the voice. Try not to do something new before an audition. If possible, invest in a professionally taken photograph (a "head shot") that presents the best possible likeness of you. Make sure your résumé is clear, concise, and truthful. Think of every audition as important—because it is.

A good audition is a singing experience where you are in control of what you want to do and do the best that you possibly can. You may not always get the role or win the competition, but if you start a pattern of good auditions, good things will eventually happen. It is important to stay with it and monitor what went well and what didn't. Remember that the audition is a learning process, as is the performance. A good book about the art of auditioning is *Complete Preparation: A Guide to Auditioning for Opera* by renowned opera coach Joan Dornemann.[1]

What do opera companies look for in an audition?

Those who spend much of their time auditioning young singers tell me that the beginning of the audition is especially crucial. This includes walking out with purpose and desire, beginning the audition in character, and making specific and clear dramatic choices. When hundreds of singers are being heard, the unique voice making interesting and possibly nonconventional choices will stand out positively. In other words, playing it safe will help you survive the experience but will not show that you have something to say. Stretch your imagination and control the space. Communicate—don't just replicate.

Since the audition package most often has you singing arias in the original language, make sure not only that you know the English translation of the words, but that you can articulate what the words mean to you. Chapter 11 should be helpful to you in preparation of your aria "plan."

Should I do a follow-up after the audition?

The relationship between you and those for whom you are auditioning does not end with the audition itself. Send a note to the auditioning organization thanking them for taking the time to hear you. Remember that they are doing you a favor by listening to you. If you are about to sing a performance somewhere, send them a notice of this. Keep them in your performing loop

1. Joan Dornemann, with Maria Ciaccia, *Complete Preparation: A Guide to Auditioning for Opera* (New York: Excalibur, 1992). Ms. Dornemann, a coach at the Metropolitan Opera, has prepared the most prominent international artists for their performances at the Met.

without being a nuisance. Do not call repeatedly or send inappropriate or long personal letters.

CONCLUSION

The advice in this chapter reflects the words and experiences of singer managers from New York, directors of important young artist programs, representatives from Opera America, and professional singers. In particular, the following individuals were kind enough to share their wisdom with the students of the Indiana University Opera Theater and the readers of this book:

- Gayletha Nichols, Met Auditions National Director, Met Young Artist Program
- Joan Dornemann, author of *Complete Preparation: A Guide to Auditioning for Opera*
- Christopher Hahn, Artistic Director, Pittsburgh Opera
- John Berry, Casting Director, English National Opera
- Ken Benson, Columbia Artists Management
- John J. Miller, Artists Manager
- Dale Johnson, Artistic Director, Minnesota Opera
- Diana Hossack, Artistic Services Director, Opera America (www. operaam.org—become a member of Opera America!)

Appendix A. Attitude Chart

Happy	Surprised	Angry	Sad
Amused	Alarmed	Angry	Apologetic
Bright	Astonished	Annoyed	Ashamed
Candid	Astounded	Argumentative	Bored
Cheerful	Awed	Arrogant	Cheerless
Comic	Breathless	Bitter	Coaxing
Compassionate	Cautious	Bold	Colorless
Confiding	Curious	Cynical	Contrite
Contented	Desperate	Disgusted	Cool
Cordial	Ecstatic	Enraged	Crushed
Deliberate	Fearful	Fierce	Disappointed
Eager	Frantic	Furious	Dismal
Elated	Frightened	Greedy	Doubting
Energetic	Hilarious	Harsh	Feeble
Enraptured	Horrified	Hateful	Hysterical
Exalted	Nervous	Indignant	Indifferent
Forgiving	Shocked	Insulting	Insane
Frank	Suspicious	Irritable	Meek
Hopeful	Terrified	Jealous	Melancholy
Impulsive	Uneasy	Mocking	Mournful
Innocent	Wary	Pompous	Pathetic
Joyful		Proud	Pitying
Jubilant		Sarcastic	Plaintive
Lively		Satiric	Pleading
Lofty		Savage	Preoccupied
Loving		Scornful	Quiet
Mild		Sharp	Resigned
Peaceful		Spiteful	Severe
Playful		Thoughtless	Shy
Pleasant			Solemn
Reverent			Sorrowful
Serene			Sour
Simple			Submissive
Sincere			Sulky
Sophisticated			Sullen
Sprightly			Timid
Sympathetic			Tragic
Tender			Troubled
Trusting			Wary
Wild			Worried

Appendix B. Postural Alignment
Emily Bogard

INTRODUCTION

Vocal training is complex; the concepts of voice, body, and mind must be developed and joined as a functioning unit. To create a vibrant, authentic vocal performance one must engage the entire self in an integrated way. This integration is developed through long and careful consideration of self-awareness and choice: bringing to consciousness how one is using the components of the "self" and making choices about whether to continue in the same way or try a new path. The manner in which choices are made can be facilitated if an attitude of open exploration is employed, while realizing that the old path is always available. The following appendix deals with alignment and many other concepts such as posture, centering, focusing, and relaxation, all valuable in the training of a performing artist.

COMING TO TERMS

Relaxation for the performing artist contributes to a state of balancing bodily tensions. It is an active rather than a passive activity of restful alertness that allows one to focus and concentrate, creating a sense of "centeredness"—the experience of the total self, a state of readiness, a source of energy.

Posture can be defined as "the position or carriage of the body or of parts of the body."[1] It can also refer to a position assumed or a mental attitude. Thus, posture can be an important consideration when exploring the physical development of characters that singers may portray. It is important to distinguish between the singer's personal posture and the posture of a character.

Alignment is "place in line; arrangement in line."[2] For the performing artist, alignment refers to the act of balancing and transferring weight through the skeletal framework to provide stability and responsiveness when executing a movement.

Poise can also be a factor when defined as "to bring into balance; support as in readiness; physical ease in bearing or movement."[3] It can be felt as a state of hovering or suspended motion.

Teachers and performers in theater have discussed these terms in both theoretical and practical applications. Robert Benedetti states our aim in aligning and centering the body is to put ourselves in the most responsive physio-vocal condition.

1. Funk and Wagnalls, *Standard College Dictionary* (New York: Harcourt, Brace & World, 1963), p. 1055.
2. Ibid., p. 36.
3. Ibid., p. 1043.

We are not interested in "correct" posture or voice, for there is no "correct" voice or posture for the actor until they are determined by the demands of his or her characterization; here we are merely working to achieve a neutral but energized condition from which we are ready to move in any way necessary to fulfill the demands of our dramatic task.[4] Jacques Lecoq trained his actors to be familiar with the "masque neuter," which was designed to rid the actor of conditioned attitudes in favor of an economical use of the body. Thus, the actor became a blank sheet of paper, a tabula rasa upon which a character could be defined who was devoid of the actor's personality, temperament, or convention. To find this neutral but energized state the performer would have to give up deeply ingrained but superficial habits.[5]

F. Matthias Alexander spoke of "the use of the self," and author Pedro de Alcantara defined the use of the self as "the way I react, with the whole of myself in any given situation."[6] Alexander encouraged his students to become aware of habitual patterns that interfered with what he referred to as "self-use." Before performers can even consider the physical development of their character (posture), they must consider their own unique structure (alignment/poise) and how consciously or unconsciously a choice is made to organize (use of the self) themselves in relationship to their environment—this is to say, self-observation in everyday activities, not just in the studio or in rehearsal, for habitual use cannot be separated from artistic technique.

In practice this means becoming aware of structural organization and how the structure functions. The use of the whole being exists between the bottom of the feet and the top of the head in response to any given stimulus. This stimulus and response may be conscious or unconscious. The bottoms of the feet align with the pull of gravity, and the top of the head extends into the vertical. Alignment is a balancing activity—a dialogue between compression and elongation of the skeletal structure. It is not a fixed position or a "right" way to stand, but rather establishing a vertical energy line around which the body parts can orient themselves.[7] This is a dynamic process that includes awareness, self-observation, understanding structural alignment and how it functions in terms of body mechanics, and the use of imagery to facilitate change.

SELF-USE: THE ALEXANDER TECHNIQUE AS BASIS FOR AWARENESS AND SELF-OBSERVATION

What follows is an all-too-brief description of the Alexander Technique. It is not possible in a short essay to do justice to this important body of work. It is possible only to introduce the work and to encourage further readings and experiences with the technique. Its importance transcends singing, bringing relief from ailments related to stress and excess muscle tension into other aspects of life.

4. Robert L. Benedetti, *The Actor at Work* (Englewood Cliffs, N.J.: Prentice-Hall, 1976), p. 27.
5. Sears Eldredge and Hollis W. Huston, "Actor Training in the Neutral Mask," in *Movement for the Actor*, ed. Lucille S. Rubin (New York: Drama Book Specialists, 1980), p. 73.
6. Pedro de Alcantara, *Indirect Procedures* (Oxford: Clarendon Press, 1997), p. 12.
7. Andrea Olsen, *Body Stories* (Tarrytown, N.Y.: Station Hill Press, 1991), p. 51.

F. Matthias Alexander was an actor who was plagued by the repeated loss of his voice. Aileen Crow in her article "The Alexander Technique as a Basic Approach to Theatrical Training" describes the background: Neither rest nor doctors could help him; consequently he undertook a long project of self-observation using three-way mirrors. He discovered that in anticipation of speaking he was pressing his head back and down, sucking in breath, depressing his larynx, lifting his chest, and compressing his spine.

Along with excessive muscular tension throughout his body, these elements constituted distortion of his entire physical-mental mechanism. He also discovered that his feelings were unreliable as a guide, for what felt natural to him was his habitual faulty response pattern. He learned to inhibit his stressful response when he felt the impulse to speak and to give himself time to direct his actions in an organized way by concentrating on the "means whereby," instead of "end gaining." In today's terminology this means he became more process- than result- or goal-oriented; he began to live in the moment, the here and now, rather than pushing to gain a goal.[8]

Alexander discovered what he called the "primary control" as the main organizer of the self. This is the dynamic relationship between our head and our neck, and the head and neck in relationship to the entire body. It is often referred to as the "head-neck-back relationship." The importance of this relationship is not in physical positioning but rather in maintaining freedom of movement between the head, neck, and back. In physiological terms it is a reflex response of the organism to gravity that integrates the other reflex systems. People commonly interfere with this mechanism through habitual, learned responses that disturb the tonic relations between the head, neck, and trunk, causing a lack of coordination and balance. Richard Brennan provides the following example: "When a rider wishes to stop a horse, he or she pulls the horse's head back with the reins. The animal immediately loses its co-ordination and soon comes to a stand still."[9] One can unconsciously rein in by setting or holding the head in a rigid pattern. When this interference is perceived kinesthetically, it can be inhibited, and the antigravity response is facilitated and its integrative effect is restored.

Students of the Alexander Technique learn to observe themselves in action and to become aware of their particular tension problems. Teachers of the technique sense potential movement in the student's body and, through a light, delicate touch, encourage the movement of energy through previously immobilized parts. This frees the flow of energy and facilitates a redistribution of body weight and a sense of the relationship between body parts. What feels "right" is often what is most familiar; so part of the work is getting comfortable with the changing sensations.[10] Students are guided to kinesthetically understand the following directions for self-use.

8. Aileen Crow, "The Alexander Technique as a Basic Approach to Theatrical Training," in Rubin, ed., *Movement for the Actor*, p. 7.
9. Richard Brennan, *The Alexander Technique Workbook* (Rockport, Mass.: Element Books, 1992), p. 7.
10. Crow, p. 8.

LET MY NECK BE FREE

(This is to eliminate the excess tension that may be present in the neck muscles.)

TO LET MY HEAD MOVE FORWARD AND UP

(The head is balanced on the spine in such a way that when the neck muscles are released the head goes slightly forward, which takes the whole body into movement. It is important to realize that the forward direction is the head going forward on the spine as if the head is nodding yes. The upward direction is away from the spine.)

TO LET MY SPINE LENGTHEN

(This direction will encourage the whole torso to lengthen toward both the head and tail. Compression is removed from the spine, and there is a sense of space between each vertebra. It is important to think of the torso three-dimensionally to avoid lengthening only the front or back of the body. Lengthening the spine is not the same as holding it straight. Holding the back flat or the spine straight reduces flexibility.)

AND MY SHOULDERS WIDEN

(There is a sense of the shoulder girdle releasing and spreading into expansion with an outward flow of energy from the center of the chest out and down through the fingertips.)

In addition one should be aware of freedom in the hip joints, the knees, and the ankles; think "space in your joints" while moving into an expansive state instead of compressive state. Thinking of the definition of poise as "to hover or suspend" creates a light, open feeling in the upper body. The image of a moving train can be used to visualize this lengthening process. The head is the engine that transmits movement to the rest of the body. Alexander's students might say, "Everything all together, one after the other."

The process of the Alexander Technique is one of awareness, inhibition, and direction. Put differently, one must first become aware of self-use or misuse, inhibit any unwanted action, and think in the directions that activate the primary control. This is mainly a process of "nondoing." De Alcantara writes, "The most prevalent cause of misuse and poor functioning is lack of inhibitory directions. Orders not to do and to stop doing should normally take precedence over directions to do."[11]

PROCESS VIA THE NEGATIVE

Technical training in the performing arts largely involves learning how to do things. Approaching alignment through the Alexander Technique means bringing to consciousness what not to do by recognizing the actions that are interfering with or blocking one's process. Theater teachers working with masks believe that training should be a *via negativa:* they will not tell the student what to do, but they will point

11. De Alcantara, p. 57.

out what not to do. "By blocking the path taken by the actor," writes Bari Rolfe, "you oblige him to look for another. Each restriction placed on the actor forces his imagination to seek ways to get around it."[12]

Alexander called this process inhibition. Richard Brennen states that Alexander realized that in order to bring about a desirable change in the use of his body he first would have to inhibit (or stop) his habitual responses to a given stimulus. By stopping for a moment before an action takes place we have time to use our reasoning powers to check which is the most efficient and appropriate way of performing such an action. This is a vital step toward having the power to choose freely on every level. If we are ever to change our habitual responses to given stimuli, we have to make a conscious decision to refuse to act in our old automatic and unconscious patterns—that is, to say "no" to our ingrained habits of use. By inhibiting our initial action we have the choice to make an entirely different decision.[13]

With technique one often needs to stop doing something in order to do what is wanted. Confusion occurs when, by adding a behavior while attempting to correct an existing unwanted behavior, a performer adopts a corrective behavior which places unnecessary tension on the physiological structure. For example, the habit of slouching forward often can result from overly shortened flexor muscles in the abdomen. This places stress on the extensor muscles of the back and results in neck, shoulder, and/or back pain. To "correct" this by tightening the extensor muscles of the back without releasing the flexors causes both sets of muscles to work against one another instead of in harmony. When the flexors release, the extensors can relax restoring balance to the torso.

Another example is dieting. A person decides to go on a diet knowing that they need to eat more fruits and vegetables, but if they only add the new foods to the existing diet of sugar and fats, weight might not be lost. First, they must inhibit the wrong eating habits, and then make a choice about what will be better nutrition.

STRUCTURE: ALIGNING THE SKELETAL SYSTEM

Alignment is the ordering of the bony structures; poise is the activity of balancing these structures. In the human body the skeleton is a system of weights and levers serving as the framework that supports the body's weight. The body is brought into balance by aligning the bones so that weight is transferred through the center of each joint from the top of the head to the bottom of the feet and then into the ground. When weight is not distributed through the center of the joint, the muscles, ligaments, and tendons surrounding the joint bear the weight, thus building stress and tension in these soft tissues. A head that hangs forward of the neck stresses the muscles of the neck and shoulders, requiring these structures to both support and move the head. When weight is transferred to the center of the joint ligaments, tendons and muscles function properly to move bones and not to support weight. The weight of a head balanced directly on top of the spine is transferred through the bony framework into the feet, allowing muscles to manipulate action of the skull.

12. Eldredge, pp. 76–77.
13. Brennan, p. 60.

Understanding how weight is supported through the skeletal system can aid the study of alignment; weight can sit upon, hang from, or be braced by a bony structure. Perform the following exercises and note any kinetic changes based on the distribution of weight.

1. Think of the head sitting lightly on top of the spine. Does this change the sensation of the weight of the head? Can it sit in a state of poise suspension as opposed to the static feeling of holding the head up or feeling its weight pressing into the neck?

2. The weight of the shoulder girdle can be perceived as sitting on the rib cage or hanging from the back of the skull. How do these two different ways of thinking change the sensation of the shoulder girdle?

3. The bracing of the femurs into the hip joint can support the weight of the pelvis with the sacrum acting as a keystone. Or the pelvis can sit on top of the legs or hang from the end of the spine. These options for organizing the weight of the pelvis can be appropriate for various activities. Walk while thinking of the pelvis as (1) hanging from the end of the spine, (2) sitting on top of your legs, and (3) being braced by the femurs. Did these various ways of thinking affect the quality of the movement? Try the same process while first standing still and then while pushing a large object.

THE THREE BONY MASSES OF THE BODY CORE

Structural alignment involves three primary body weights: the skull, the thorax (rib cage), and pelvis, all organized around a vertical plumb line. Our high center of gravity is delicately balanced over our base of support, the feet.[14] Because the body connects to the earth through the feet, work on alignment begins from the ground up, with each body part balanced in sequence.

To make changes in alignment it is necessary to sense the shifting of body weight through the joints. Notice how subtle shifts cause a redistribution of weight and how the accompanying tension on muscles provides clues to approaching a state of equilibrium and poise.

THE FEET: THE FOUNDATION

A state of balance must begin with a strong foundation. In the body the feet are the "footers" providing the connection and grounding to the earth that is necessary for efficient movement. Relaxation of the feet and ankles is essential for a sense of grounding. This yielding allows the soft tissue to receive the weight of the upper body and respond with an oppositional thrust through the joints, moving the bony structure into a vertical alignment.

1. Imagine the soles of the feet spreading into the floor, soft pads like a cat's paw, while the ankles remain resilient, spongelike connectors between the feet and legs. As the weight presses into the ground, the foot and ankle spread and then spring back as the weight is released.

2. Standing with feet about twelve to eighteen inches apart and the heels in line

14. Olsen, p. 50.

with the toes, notice where the weight rests through the feet. Is it toward the toes, heels, inside or outside of the feet? Does the distribution of weight feel the same in both feet or different from the right or left? Shift the weight forward from the ankle joints (not forward through the pelvis, chest, or head). Go to the point just before a loss of balance and notice what muscles are working to hold this off-balance position. Reverse this process to the back, noting any muscular holding. Now shift the weight from front to back, decreasing the amount of movement with each shift until the muscular effort to remain in a standing position is minimal and a balanced neutral home base is attained. Notice any changes in the distribution of weight through the feet. In general, for an active standing alignment the weight should pass through the ball of the foot, creating a state of readiness, poised for movement. When the weight rests back onto the heels, a shift of weight forward must occur before any movement can begin.

THE KNEES: MOVING ON UP

The balancing act continues through the knee joint with the knees being free, neither locked nor bent. A common malpractice of some "postural" classes has been to ask students to bend their knees to release the lower back. This bent-knee position is a holding pattern that can cause the pelvis to tuck under, pulling the spine into a C-shaped curve with the head forward of the neck. Conversely, locking the knee joint can result in a deepening of the lumbar curve and over-extending the chest.

THE PELVIS: THE FIRST BONY MASS

Poised on top of the legs or hanging from the spine at the interface with the sacrum is the pelvis. This large bony mass functions as a basin to hold and protect the organs and soft tissue of the abdomen. The organization of the pelvis has a direct effect on the entire spine and the use of the lower limbs. Any tilt forward or backward or twist to one side can create tension in the structures above and below the pelvis, especially through the lumbar spine.

Imagine that the pelvis is a bowl of water filled to within an inch of the brim. Allow the water to gently slosh from front to back without spilling out the front or the back. Any excessive anterior or posterior tilt of the pelvis will cause distortions in the alignment of the upper body. Finding a neutral balance for the pelvis will echo the sensations of Alexander's primary control for the head, because both the head and pelvis are balanced freely on each end of the spine.

Singers need to be aware of the pelvic floor, a nest of muscles between the legs and from the pubic bone to tailbone that weave a closure for the bottom of the pelvis. An inner unit of the transverse abdominus, the multifidi (back extensors) and the pelvic floor provide deep support of the breath and stabilization of the pelvis during inhalation and exhalation.

A common misuse of the pelvis is to tuck under. As in the bent-knee position, the top of the pelvis tilts backward, curving the tailbone under, pulling down on the upper body, collapsing the chest, and bringing the head forward. Releasing the pelvis from the tuck lengthens the hamstring muscles and the front abdominal wall.

This opens the upper body, freeing the lower end of the sternum and allowing the head to find its balance point.

THE RIB CAGE: THE SECOND BONY MASS

The rib cage exists in three dimensions with each rib acting as a louver on the spine. During inhalation the rib cage expands forward, backward and sideways and rises only slightly. The rib cage can be viewed as a large oval suspended from the spine and enclosed on the front by the sternum. Any directional shift of the rib cage affects the thoracic vertebra and the head.

Experience what happens to the head and spine when the weight of the rib cage is shifted as follows:

Drop the base of the sternum down and back.
Lift the base of the sternum forward and up.
Move the base of the sternum from side to side.
Try all of the above, initiating movement from the top of the sternum.

A neutral balance of the rib cage evokes a feeling of the rib cage sliding down over a lengthening upward movement of the front abdominal wall.

THE SKULL: THE THIRD BONY MASS

The skull (the final bony mass) weighs ten to fifteen pounds and sits atop the spine; its balance is crucial to efficient movement function as described in the Alexander Technique. The skull sits upon the first vertebra (the atlas) via two little "rockers" called the condyles, which are bony protuberances of the occipital lobe. These rockers interface with the concave receptacles of the atlas, allowing the skull to rock back and forth as in nodding yes. The atlas sitting upon the second vertebra (the axis) allows the head to pivot from right to left. Noninterference with the balance of the skull (on the atlas) and the atlas (on the axis) keeps the reflex of our primary control functioning.

1. Experiencing movement around the axes passing through the head can help to sense the balance of the head on the spine.

Place your fingers lightly in the ears and rotate the head as if saying yes. This is movement around the horizontal axis.

Place one finger on the top of the head and rotate the head as if saying no. This is movement around the vertical axis.

Place one finger at the bridge of the nose and tilt the head from side to side. This is movement around the saggittal axis.

Visualize the place in the center of the skull where these three axes intersect. This intersection is the point of balance for the skull sitting on top of the spine. This point is deep in the center of the skull about ear level.

2. Imagine a horizontal plate sitting at this point with the spine supporting the plate. Circle the plate as a juggler who balances plates on a long stick. Next place a marble on the plate and roll the marble around the center of the plate. Notice any point where the marble might be inclined to roll off the plate. When singing, the

balance of the head should remain free; there should be no setting of the primary control—the marble should move freely without falling off the plate.

3. To bring awareness to the back of the skull, look to the right by shifting the back of the head forward to the left. Look to the left by shifting the back of the head forward to the right. Look down by moving the back of the head up, and look up by moving the back of the head down. The muscles that move the skull attach on the back side. The movement from the back side creates activity behind the ears, providing freedom for the head/neck area.

4. Imagine a mouth on the back of the skull at the base; put a smile there, yawn.

5. Think of separating the base of the skull from the neck and visualize the back of the skull splitting in half vertically, with the weight falling forward into the jaw and continuing to exit through the chin.

THE SPINE: THE CONNECTOR

The spine is a series of alternating curves beginning with the anterior cervical (neck) curve, into the posterior thoracic (back of the rib cage), followed by the anterior lumbar (lower back) curve, and finally the posterior sacral curve made up of the sacrum and coccyx (tailbone). The focus of alignment is to bring these opposing curves into balance to provide a responsive state of stability and mobility and to serve as a shock absorber for vital organs. The three-dimensional mobility of the spine allows forward, backward, sideways, and twisting movement. The stability of the spine provides a framework for the muscles and fascia. The goal is a lengthened spine, not a "straight" spine—a spine allowing lightness and freedom in the upper body for manipulation of the environment, and the grounding and stability of the lower body to move through space. The spine connects the three bony masses, and since the body is a closed system, each of these structures has an effect upon each of the others.

QUALITY OF MOVEMENT

Movement is the key to balance, and the quality of movement determines whether one is in a state of neutral balance or a state of hyper- or hypotension. Alignment is not a position or a place. The human body is never truly still; even in sleep there is constant movement within. This continual act of balance for daily activities requires subtle weight shifts in the joints by means of light, delicate movements.

Imagine balancing an egg on end. Use the hand to mime this activity, noticing the quality and the manner of movement. With the hand hovering over the top of the egg, lightly touch the egg, and with small, delicate movements sense the shifting of the egg's weight. Feel the weight of the egg balanced through its center, and gently, with a sense of suspension, release the hand.

This is the manner for approaching the organizational alignment of the bony structure. Any use of force to push or pull oneself into a position only will create unnecessary tension. The joints provide the freedom for movement, the bones provide the transfer of weight, and the muscles are the articulators that allow the utterances of movement expressions.

ALIGNMENT EXPERIMENT TO FEEL THE DYNAMIC PULLS TOWARD GRAVITY AND VERTICALITY: THE BODY CORE

Standing in a slightly collapsed posture, feel the heaviness of the three bony masses (the head, the thorax, and the pelvis), noticing the support for each of these weights. This is a passive state. Feel the impulse to move into a more vertical stance, bringing attention to the feet, softening the ankles, allowing the bottom of the feet to spread into the floor, and shifting the weight into the balls of the feet. Wiggle the toes, and with light movements move the bones in the feet while maintaining connection with the ground. This is an activity of yielding. Gently, but firmly, press the feet into the ground as if stepping to activate an automated doormat. Pressing through the soles of the feet initiates an oppositional movement though the arches of the feet. The movement continues up the lower leg, releasing the knees, traveling up the inner thigh into the hip sockets. The impulse from each leg joins at the front of the sacrum, releasing the pelvis as the movement continues up the *front* of the spine, lengthening the abdominal muscles and allowing space to circulate between each vertebra. The rib cage eases as the movement passes underneath the sternum along the *front* of the thoracic vertebra. Continue to allow space to circulate around these vertebrae as the movement continues along the *front* of the cervical vertebra and exits out each ear and the top of the head.

This is an experience of the body core. The energy from the feet pressing into the floor and moving through the body core is the dynamic push/pull that supports verticality. The power of the feet and the freedom of the head allows for function in the space between. Alignment of the body weight in conjunction with the manifestation of energy through muscular effort establishes self-use.

ENERGY: THE FUEL FOR OUR ALIGNMENT

The word "energy" is often used in describing a person's performance—"his stage presence was filled with vibrant energy." The energy to practice, rehearse, or perform can be evasive. But what exactly is energy? How does one access and manipulate this source of vitality, and how does this manifest itself in the quality of our movement and alignment?

Energy can be defined as "the vigor or intensity of action, expression, or utterance; or the capacity for overcoming inertia."[15] This can be an active state or the potential for action. Effort can be defined as "the force exerted against the inertia of a body";[16] flow refers to how we are using our energy. Other words such as power, force, and vigor are all effects of our ability to act.

Rudolph von Laban states that effort refers to the inner impulses or drives of an individual from which movement originates. These impulses are visibly expressed in the rhythms of a person's bodily motion, the way they use their movement energy. Laban described movement quality as being reflections of inner attitudes which may or may not be willful, but which are always present in the alive human

15. Funk and Wagnalls, p. 437.
16. Ibid., p. 422.

body. Effort flow deals with the relationship of control to fluidity and is described in terms of a range from free to bound.[17]

Free flow is an expansive use of energy. Bound flow is a condensed use of energy. In all movement there is a constant adjustment of our body weight experienced as a range from light to strong, in a time range from sustained to sudden, occurring in direct to indirect spatial pathways. This activity is an interplay between freeness and boundness.

In physiological terms, energy is a metabolic process based on the consumption of calories and the burning of calories. All the nutritional and healthful activities one participates in affect energy production.

But beyond this metabolic activity, energy is an outward expression of internal impulses, conscious or unconscious, affected by emotional and spiritual states. In *The Actor at Work* Robert Benedetti speaks about the flow of action into activity:

> Once the choice to act has been made and the aroused energy becomes a purposeful intention or point of reaction, it changes modes from the internal to the external and becomes an activity. Notice however that it retains the vitality of the original stimulus. The activity "to get a drink" is really the outer or public form of the inner action, "to quench my thirst"; they each describe a different phase of the same energy. Defined in this way, our external activities become total gestures arising from deep personal energies, and those objects or relationships involved in our activities become endowed with a deeply personal quality—they become extensions of us, for the whole process of action from stimulus to event is literally your inside becoming your outside. Your full sense of your action must encompass this entire process, so that your defined action is not a static image but is rather a name for an experienced flow of energy.[18]

The "experienced flow of energy" pertinent to this chapter is alignment. To experience alignment as a deep body core activity is to sense the energy of an inner impulse as an interplay between free and bound flow manipulating Laban's effort factors, using weight in a light, sustained, indirect manner. To work externally with strong, quick, direct movements to align the body core could lead to putting oneself in superficially held positions.

A WORD ABOUT TENSION

Tension is often thought about in a negative sense, but tension is needed in the body to provide an active but stabile state. De Alcantara wrote,

> When somebody complains of tension, he really means too much tension, or more precisely, the wrong kind and amount of tension, in the wrong places, for the wrong length of time. In itself tension is not negative. . . . The cause of wrong tension is most often the lack of right tension. In such cases it is fruitless to try to relax these wrong tensions directly; the solution lies in creating the right tensions, and letting relaxation come about on its own. Right tension usu-

17. Cecily Dell, *A Primer for Movement Description Using Effort-Shape and Supplementary Concepts* (New York: Dance Notation Bureau Press, 1977), pp. 13–14.
18. Benedetti, p. 205.

ally involves proper muscular initiation and sequencing through the balancing of muscle action on each side of the joint.[19]

Doris Humphery, noted choreographer and dancer, described movement as an arc between two deaths, one side being total collapse where no muscular tension exists, and the other side being total rigidity where too much tension creates a state of immobility. In the middle is home base, a neutral balanced place of dynamic potential enabling one to move in any desired direction. As the pendulum swings from one side to the other, one can begin to distinguish the "right tension" needed for a specific activity, not too much, not too little, but just right.

Lie on the floor in a collapsed state. Feel the impulse to come to a standing position, noticing what muscles are being engaged and how weight is being shifted. Continue to move to the vertical with awareness of passing through a home base. Continue on, tightening muscles into a state of total rigidity. Reverse the process, returning to the floor. Note the organization of muscle, bone, and weight throughout this activity as a result of the impulse to stand.

TO REVIEW

In summary, the use of the self when working with alignment requires an integrated merger of the body and mind responding to and acting upon internal impulses, resulting in a balance of the bony framework through the subtle shifting of body weight. The process of the Alexander Technique encourages one to become aware of habitual use, choose to inhibit unwanted actions, and engage the primary control. Through the use of Alexander's directions one can establish a neutral alignment of the body core: the spine connecting the head, rib cage, and pelvis with the feet supporting and transferring the weight of the body into the ground. The response to inner impulses is the external activity of small, light, delicate movements shifting joints and bringing muscle groups into balance, promoting a lengthened and expansive state of the body structure.

19. De Alcantara, p. 15.

Appendix C. Literary and Historical Background of Selected Operas

The literary and historical excerpts in Appendix C are just a few examples of the many source materials that have inspired operatic works. Novels, plays, and historical materials often describe characters and setting in a level of detail that is impossible in an opera. These types of materials can assist the singer in composing a character profile by helping him or her understand the character's intentions in the opera. When used in conjunction with the exercises in Chapters 4 and 12, this type of research can result in a greater range of choices for the singer.

As you read through the different types of analysis in this appendix, note how some excerpts highlight characterization (*La Bohème*), while others focus on the details of the historical setting (*Les Dialogues des Carmélites*). By comparing source materials with an opera, you can often "fill in the blanks" of key scenes (*La Traviata*) and supporting roles. Source material can also provide a new perspective on a character (*Carmen*) or a different point of view on a story (*Madama Butterfly*). Finally, by researching the historical setting of an opera or source material (*Tosca*), one can create a rich and accurate context in which to place his or her character.

Carmen by Georges Bizet

Drawn from the novella *Carmen* by Prosper Mérimée

Singers can often find their character's "voice" in literary sources. Prosper Mérimée was born in Paris in 1803 and wrote plays, a novel, and short stories after he completed his law studies. In 1854 he was appointed a senator and became a prominent figure at the court of Napoleon III. He wrote the novella *Carmen* in 1846. The short story is storytelling at its best, with clear descriptions of Don José and Carmen. In this excerpt from the novella, the singer can discover something about Don José's background and point of view. Speaking directly to the reader, Don José introduces himself and describes his reaction when he sees Carmen for the first time:

> If I call myself don, it is because I am entitled to do so, and if we were in Elizondo I would show you my genealogy on parchment. They wanted me to go into the church, and I was given some schooling, but little good did it do me. I was too fond of playing pelota, that was my undoing. When we Navarrese play pelota we don't spare a thought for anything else. Once when I'd won a game, a lad from Alava province picked a quarrel with me. We picked up our maquilas [iron tipped sticks used by the Basques], and once again I was the victor; but I had to leave the province as a result. I met up with some dragoons and en-

listed in the Almansa Cavalry Regiment. We mountain folk are quick to learn military ways. I soon became a corporal, and had already been promised promotion to sergeant when it was my misfortune to be put on guard at the cigar factory in Seville.

As you know, señor, around four or five hundred women work in the factory. They roll the cigars in a room in which men aren't allowed without a pass from the magistrate, because when it's hot the girls don't believe in over-dressing. . . . I raised my head, and saw her. It was a Friday; I'll never forget it. I saw Carmen, whom you know, and at whose place we met a few months ago. . . .

She was wearing a very short red skirt, beneath which you could see her white silk stockings with holes in them and dainty red morocco-leather shoes fastened with flame-colored ribbons. Her mantilla was parted so as to reveal her shoulders and a big bunch of acacia flowers which she had in the front of her blouse. She had another acacia bloom in one corner of her mouth, and she moved forward swaying her hips like some filly out of the Cordoba stud. In my part of the world everyone would have crossed themselves at the sight of a woman dressed like that; but there in Seville everyone paid her some risqué compliment on her appearance. She replied to them all, eyeing them archly, with her fist on her hip, brazen like the true Gypsy she was. At first I didn't find her attractive, and I returned to my task; but, acting as women and cats usually do, refusing to come when they are called, but coming when they are not called, she stopped in front of me. . . . And taking the acacia flower from her mouth, she flicked it at me with her thumb, right between the eyes. Señor, it was like a bullet hitting me. I didn't know where to hide myself, I stood there like a block of wood. When she had gone into the factory, I saw the acacia flower that had fallen to the ground at my feet. I don't know what came over me, but I picked it up without my companions noticing and tucked it away in my tunic for safe keeping. That was my first piece of folly![1]

La Traviata by Verdi

DRAWN FROM THE NOVEL AND PLAY LA DAME AUX CAMÉLIAS BY ALEXANDRE DUMAS FILS

La Dame aux camélias (The Lady of the Camellias) was a popular, middle-class novel, later turned into a play, based on an actual person of the time. The story, contemporary with Verdi's 1848 opera, was in form a narration from the pen of Armand (Alfredo). The novel thoroughly describes the characters that become Violetta, Alfredo, and Germont in the opera, La Traviata. One can easily see how the words used in the novel to describe Marguerite (Violetta Valery) inspired the musical agitation of her opening aria ("Senza libera") in the opera: "This hilarity, this way of talking and drinking, which seemed to me in the others the mere results of bad company or of bad habits, seemed in Marguerite a necessity of forgetting, a fever, a nervous irritability."[2]

1. Prosper Mérimée, *Carmen and Other Stories*, trans. Nicholas Jotcham (New York: Oxford University Press, 1989), p. 20.

2. Alexandre Dumas *fils*, *Camille, the Lady of the Camellias*, trans. Edmond Gosse (New York: Signet Classics, 1984), p. 82.

The book also supplies a missing piece of the puzzle of act 2 of the opera. In the novel, the character of Armand's (Alfredo's) father, Germont, confronts the character of Marguerite (Violetta) and alludes to the possibility of a jealous Armand being killed by a man from her past:

> You love Armand; prove it to him by the sole means which remains to you of yet proving it to him, by sacrificing your love to his future. No misfortune has yet arrived, but one will arrive, and perhaps a greater one than those which I foresee. Armand might become jealous of a man who has loved you; he might provoke him, fight, and be killed. Think, then, what you would suffer in the presence of a father who should call on you to render an account for the life of his son![3]

In the opera, Violetta raises this specter by taunting Alfredo in the card scene (act 2, scene 2).

Falstaff by Giuseppe Verdi

DRAWN FROM *HENRY IV*, PARTS ONE AND TWO, AND *THE MERRY WIVES OF WINDSOR* BY WILLIAM SHAKESPEARE

Sometimes a character in an opera is drawn from more than one theatrical source. In the opera *Falstaff*, the character of Falstaff is drawn from three plays by William Shakespeare, richly detailing a character who is more than a fat clown. Seen from the perspective of all of the plays, Falstaff emerges as witty and clever.

The "fat knight" as created by Arrigo Boito is a brilliant combination of the humorous clown of Shakespeare's *Merry Wives of Windsor* with the man of wit found in the *Henry IV* plays. In act 2, scene 5 of *Henry IV, Part One* is found the line "Go thy ways, old Jack," reused in the monologue for Falstaff that Boito and Verdi placed at the beginning of act 3. In response to Prince Hal's asking Falstaff when it last was that Falstaff was svelte enough to see his own knee, Falstaff's rejoinder, "When I was about thy years, Hal, I was not an eagle's talon in the waist; I could have crept into any alderman's thumb ring," was doubtless part of the inspiration for Falstaff's arietta in act 2, "Quand' ero paggio."[4] Perhaps most revealing in Shakespeare is Falstaff's description of himself: "A goodly portly man, I' faith, and a corpulent; of a cheerful look, a pleasing eye, and a most noble carriage; and, as I think, his age some fifty, or, by'r Lady, inclining to threescore; and now I remember me, his name is Falstaff."[5]

The "honor" monologue in the opera (act 1) is extracted from act 5, scene 2 of *Henry IV, Part One*:

> What is honour? A word. What is in that word "honour"? What is that "honour"? Air. A trim reckoning! Who hath it? He that died o' Wednesday. Doth he feel it? No. Doth he hear it? No. 'Tis insensible, then? Yea, to the dead. But

---

3. Ibid., p. 232.
4. William Shakespeare, *Henry IV, Part One*, ed. David Bevington (New York: Bantam Books, 1988), p. 46.
5. Ibid., p. 49.

will it not live with the living? No. Why? Detraction will not suffer it. Therefore I'll none of it. Honour is a mere scutcheon. And so ends my catechism.[6]

La Bohème by Giacomo Puccini

DRAWN FROM THE NOVEL *SCÈNES DE LA VIE DE BOHÈME* BY HENRI MÜRGER

Mürger published the novel *Scènes de la vie de bohème* (Scenes from Bohemian Life) in a Parisian magazine between 1845 and 1848; it was first issued in book form in 1851. The novel is a collection of vignettes that describe characters and their adventures in the French Quarter of Paris. In the opera, *La Bohème*, we do not meet the character of Musetta until act 2. By reading the novel, a singer can flesh out her character's (Musette) prehistory, bringing a fully developed characterization to her introductory aria, "Quando m'en vo'":

> Mademoiselle Musette was an attractive twenty-year-old girl, who, a short time after her arrival in Paris, had become what pretty girls do become when they have a fine body, lots of coquetry, some ambition, and no spelling. After having been the joy of suppers in the Latin Quarter for a long time, where she had made a name for herself by singing with a voice continually fresh, if not always true, rustic table songs, which the finest connoisseurs of rhymes have since praised, Mademoiselle Musette suddenly left the rue de la Harpe to go to live on the Cytherean heights of the Breda Quarter. She was not slow in becoming one of the queens of the aristocracy of pleasure and little by little made her way toward that goal of fame which consists in being mentioned in the Paris newspapers or having one's pictures on sale at all print dealers.

> However, Mademoiselle Musette was an exception to the women among whom she lived. It was her nature, instinctively refined and poetic, like all women who are truly women, to love luxury and all the pleasures luxury brings in its wake. Her coquetry had flaming desires for whatever was beautiful and distinguished; daughter of the people, she had never once been out of her element in the midst of the most regal splendors. But Mademoiselle Musette, who was young and beautiful, would never be the mistress of a man who was not as young and handsome as she. She had been once seen refusing courageously the splendid offers of an old man, so rich that he was called the Peru of the Chaussee d'Antin, and he had built a gold stairway for Musette's whimsical feet. Sensible feet. Sensible and clever, she had a horror of fools and simpletons whatever their age, title, or name. She was a fine and beautiful girl was this Musette, who in love adopted in part the famous epigram of Champfort: Love is the interchange of two whims. Furthermore, never had her liaisons been preceded by one of those shameful bargains which dishonor modern chivalry. As she said herself, Musette played fair and demanded that she be paid in the currency of sincerity.

> But if her whims were violent and sudden, they were never sufficiently lasting to reach the pitch of passion. And the great elasticity of her feelings, the little attention she paid to the purses, and to the rank of those who wished to court her, gave a great mobility to her life, which was perpetually alternating between

6. Ibid., p. 95.

blue coupes and omnibuses, mezzanines and the fifth floor, silk gowns and Indian cotton dresses.[7]

Don Giovanni by Wolfgang Amadeus Mozart

DRAWN FROM VARIOUS SOURCES

Lorenzo da Ponte's libretto for *Don Giovanni* drew inspiration from a number of sources in which the Don Juan figure appeared. Don Juan's adventures may have first been depicted by traveling commedia dell'arte troupes. Other sources featuring Don Juan include *El Burlador de Sevilla* by Tirso de Molina (1630), *Le Festin de Pierre* by Molière (1665), *Don Giovanni Tenorio* by Goldoni (1736), and the libretto *Don Giovanni Tenorio* written by Bertati for Gazzaniga (1775). It has even been suggested that the elderly Casanova, who documented his past adventures in his memoirs and was a friend of Da Ponte's, also contributed to the libretto.

Depending on the cultural context of the source, one can approach the physical and emotional characterization of Don Giovanni in various ways. For example, taking the twelve volumes of Casanova's memoirs at face value, one could infer that the operatic Don (like Casanova) was in the autumn of his career. How else could he, as Leporello proudly recounts to Donna Elvira, have conquered 1,003 women by this time if he had not been more "mature"? If the character is viewed from this perspective, the frustration and desperation of the aging Don can be communicated both physically and emotionally by the singer.

Source material can provide clues not only to character, but to staging as well. The play by Molina (*El Burlador de Sevilla*) provides insight into an important symbol in the opening scene of the opera. In the play Donna Anna allows Don Giovanni into her room because he is disguised as Don Ottavio; however, she recognizes that his are not the hands of Don Ottavio. Following this approach, one can explore the importance of hands to our culture and to this opera. The handshake, for example, is a symbol of trust. One can argue that the betrayal of trust is Giovanni's greatest sin—not that he seduces women, but that he gains their trust and then lies to them. The symbol of the hand as a purveyor of trust is invoked in the act 1, scene 3 aria "La cí darem la mano" (Give me your hand). This symbolism could be extended when, later in the opera, Donna Anna recognizes the Don as the man who was trying to rape her the night her father was killed (before her aria "Or sai chi l'onore"). The scene could be staged so that the Don offers her his hand before he exits. This imagery continues to the climax of the opera, when the statue of the Commendatore offers the Don his hand.

Il Barbiere de Siviglia by Gioachino Rossini

DRAWN FROM THE PLAY LE BARBIER DE SEVILLE BY PIERRE-AUGUSTIN CARON DE BEAUMARCHAIS

Rossini's opera is based like Mozart's *Le Nozze di Figaro* on a play in Beaumarchais's trilogy about the adventurer Figaro. The play, *Le Barbier de Seville*, which

7. Henri Mürger, *Scènes de la vie de bohème*, trans. Elizabeth Ward Hugus (Westport, Conn.: Hyperion Press, 1978), p. 66.

premiered in 1775, included songs with rhyming verse. The conversion of it into an opera utilizes the longer speeches, transposing them to arias. The play is helpful in capturing the mercurial spirit of Figaro as he bounces between gay wit and creative scheming. The differences between the play and the opera include the fact that in the play Figaro lives in a house that belongs to Dr. Bartolo. He lives there free of charge, but in return he is on call to be his barber, surgeon, and apothecary. In the play (act 1, scene 4), Figaro's own description of Bartolo is revealing: "He's a fine portly, squat, young old codger, grey in patches, scratchy, shaven craven, spying, prying and whining all at the same time. . . . [Bartolo is] brutish, mean, infatuated, and wildly jealous of his ward, who hates him to death."[8]

The spirit of the play in general resembles the style of the opera. Played for fun, situations and scenes are closer to farce than to the three-dimensional human profiles found in *Le Marriage de Figaro*, which premiered nine years later. Even so, there are a couple of lines that reveal the complexity of Figaro's character in the play. When the Count sarcastically asks of Figaro after a particularly bitter speech in act 1, scene 2, "Who has given you such a cheerful philosophy?" Figaro answers, "My loyal companion Misfortune. I make a point of laughing at everything, for fear of having to cry."[9]

Another revealing comment is made by Bartolo, a member of the ancien régime, pointing a barb at the new age of Enlightenment:

Rosine. You are always insulting this poor century of ours.
Bartholo: Pardon me for living! What has it produced that we should praise it for? Idiocies of every variety: freedom of thought, the laws of gravity, electricity, religious tolerationism, vaccination, quinine, the Encyclopedia, and plays . . .[10]

Le Nozze de Figaro by Wolfgang Amadeus Mozart

DRAWN FROM THE PLAY *LE MARRIAGE DE FIGARO* BY BEAUMARCHAIS

The dramatic "hinge," labeled the "moment of crisis" by Figaro in *Le Marriage de Figaro*, is a particularly revealing speech presented in act 5, scene 3. Some of the lines reflect Figaro's fourth-act aria in the opera, "Aprite po quegli occhi." But Figaro's aria in the opera draws on only a few of the lines of the play, underlining his jealousy and feelings of inadequacy. In *Le Marriage de Figaro* a politically motivated tirade exposes many of Figaro's philosophies. The key lines that underscore his attitude are these as he speaks of Count Almaviva: "Because you are a great Lord, you think your talents are infinite! . . . Nobility, fortune, rank, influence: they all make a man so proud! What have you ever done to earn such wealth? You took the trouble to be born, and that's the sum total of your efforts."[11]

---

8. Pierre-Augustin Caron de Beaumarchais, *Le Barbier de Seville*, trans. Graham Anderson (Bath: Absolute Press, 1993), p. 22.

9. Ibid., p. 18.

10. Ibid., p. 19.

11. Pierre-Augustin Caron de Beaumarchais, *Le Marriage de Figaro*, trans. Graham Anderson (Bath: Absolute Press, 1993), p. 226.

Tosca by Giacomo Puccini

DRAWN FROM THE PLAY *LA TOSCA* BY VICTORIEN SARDOU

Even though an opera may be drawn from a literary or theatrical source, that source may be set in a historical context or feature historical figures. Sardou's play *La Tosca* is set in Rome in the year 1800. It incorporates many historical details and reflects political and religious conflicts of the time. One cannot truly appreciate the conflicts in the opera and play without knowing something of the historical background.

Key to this conflict was the power vacuum created by the absence of a pope in Rome at the time that the action takes place. Cardinal Giovanni Braschi (Pius VI) became pope in 1775 and enjoyed the longest reign by a pope in the eighteenth century. He died in 1799, a prisoner of the French. The next pope, Barnaba Chiaramonti (Pius VII), became pope in March 1800. However, the Austrians prevented him from returning to Rome, and he did not arrive until four months after the election.

Into this historical setting are placed the characters of Tosca, Cavaradossi, and Scarpia. Sardou's play provides information about each character that we are not privy to in Puccini's opera. First, Cavaradossi is not an itinerant painter; since he is painting this work in the church for free, he most likely does not have to paint for a living: "I petitioned the Canons of this church for permission to paint this mural free of charge." Gennarino, Cavaradossi's assistant in the play, also gives us information about the painter: "He is a Roman just like you and me, and from an old patrician family to boot."[12] The play also outlines the relationship between Mario and Tosca:

> As a performer she is incomparable, but as a woman . . . ah, what a woman . . . !
> And to think that this exquisite creature was discovered in the fields, running
> wild, looking after some goats. . . .[13] She loves me deeply enough! She has only
> one fault: a fierce jealousy which somewhat troubles our happiness. And there
> is also her excessive piety. But love and piety can be reconciled.[14]

The play also provides important information about Scarpia: "Behind a façade of gentility and pious devotion to religion, behind smiles and signs of the cross, lurks a vicious, decadent and rotten scoundrel. He's an artist of villainy, refined in his wickedness, casual in his cruelty, bloodthirsty even in his pleasures. What wife, what daughter, what sister has come in contact with this filthy satyr and not paid for it with her honor?"[15]

Madama Butterfly by Giacomo Puccini

DRAWN FROM THE PLAY *MADAME BUTTERFLY* BY DAVID BELASCO

The opera *Madama Butterfly* is based on a short play by David Belasco which premiered in New York in March 1900. The English debut came one month later

---

12. Victorien Sardou, *La Tosca*, trans. W. Laird Kleine-Ahlbrandt (New York: Edwin Mellen Press, 1990), p. 29.
13. Ibid., p. 42.
14. Ibid., p. 43.
15. Ibid., p. 40.

in London, with Puccini in the audience. One of the main attractions of the play was to transport the audience to Nagasaki, Japan, an exotically popular locale. The first production of *Madama Butterfly* produced in America was sung in English in New York in 1907.

The play is saturated in realistic detail. The opening description of Butterfly's house describes everything in the scene to be Japanese except for the American locks and bolts on the doors and windows and an American flag fastened to a tobacco jar. While the Puccini opera opens with Pinkerton being shown the house by the Japanese "used car salesman" Goro, the play approaches the story from a Japanese point of view. In the play the first character we see on stage is Madame Butterfly, laying flowers on a shrine, then kneeling in ritualistic prayer. At the shrine lies a sword. We quickly find out that Butterfly is running out of money, and that she does not want anyone speaking Japanese in "Lef-ten-ant Pik-ker-ton's house."

Some of the most revealing information we receive from the play is about Butterfly herself: she used to be a geisha, and her honorable father died by his own sword, on which was inscribed the words "To die with honor, when one no longer can live with honor."[16] The rich Yamadori's part is also fleshed out in more detail in the play. He is very articulate in asking for the hand of Butterfly in marriage. The part of Goro is based on a character named Nakodo, who is less insensitive than Goro.

Apart from the opening act, the opera is fairly faithful to the play. The major difference is the focus on Pinkerton and his penchant for breaking into arias about himself after Sharpless (the American consul) arrives. His declared passion for the child/woman Cio-Cio San and their love duet at the end of act 1 give a decidedly Italian, and romantic, twist to the first act. In the play Pinkerton arrives with his wife Kate only in the last five pages, arriving to take the child and leave money. He gives the envelope of money to Sharpless, who in turn gives it to Butterfly "in remembrance of their past." Kate, in meeting Cio-Cio San, calls her "you pretty little plaything."

Les Dialogues des Carmélites by François Poulenc

DRAWN FROM HISTORICAL AND LITERARY SOURCES, PRINCIPALLY FROM GEORGES BERNANOS'S PLAY OF THE SAME NAME

Poulenc's *Les Dialogues des Carmélites* (The Dialogues of the Carmelites) combines fact and fiction in interesting ways. The Carmelite Martyrs of Compiègne was a community of nuns established in 1641. The community was renowned for its fervor and fidelity to St. Teresa of Avila and dedicated to prayer. It continued to enjoy the esteem of the French court, and so, a century and a half later, it became an object of hatred to the leaders of the French Revolution. As the Revolution progressed, the nuns realized the danger of their situation. In 1792 the community of twenty-one nuns offered themselves to God as a sacrifice to "placate the anger of God, so that divine peace would return to the Church and to the state."

The new Assembly, asserting its antireligious bias, proclaimed the vows taken by the religious as null and void. In 1790 the community was interviewed by local

---

16. David Belasco, *Madame Butterfly* (Boston: Little, Brown, 1928), p. 32.

government agents, who offered the nuns full freedom from their "so-called vows" with a suitable pension should they wish to leave the convent. They all refused this offer. A formal document was sent to the District Directory signed by each nun stating that they all wished to live and die as professed Carmelite nuns.

The sisters were tried and condemned to death. They were executed on the guillotine on July 17, 1794. The first to die was the novice Constance, and the Prioress was given the option of being the last to die. She mounted the scaffold singing the *Salve Regina* until her voice was silenced. Sixteen nuns died, so there were other sisters who escaped death, providing additional historical documentary information.

It was not until 1906 that the Carmelite Martyrs of Compiègne were beatified by Pope Pius X. In 1931 the novel *Song at the Scaffold* by Gertrude von Le Fort told the story in fictional form.[17] This work inspired R. Bruckberger to produce a film on the subject, and in 1937 he entrusted the writing of the dialogue to well-known writer George Bernanos.

Even though Bernanos died before perfecting the work, it was published in 1949 and met with enormous public success as a play. Many believe that Bernanos's painful and drawn-out death while writing the work was not unlike the pain, crisis of faith, and ultimate death of the Prioress in act 1 of the opera.[18]

The text of the opera is directly taken from the Bernanos play, but much had to be left out of the opera libretto. The music gives shape to a number of important speeches, including Blanche's testimony of faith to her father and the new Prioress's opening speech to the nuns. At the beginning of the opera the Marquis refers to the death of his wife, Blanche's mother, and the visions of the panicked crowd from his standpoint. Bernanos's prologue tells the story from the third person in more detail. Further on in scene 1, Blanche clearly articulates her reasons for wanting to become a nun. The stage directions state, "She speaks with sudden decision, as if in forcing herself to convince her father she were gradually giving way to the hope of convincing herself":[19]

> The weakness of my nature is not merely a humiliation which He imposes on me, but the sign of His Will in His poor handmaid. Far from feeling the shame of it, I should rather be tempted to find glory in such a destiny.

> There are several kinds of courage. One is certainly to face musket fire bravely. Another is to sacrifice the advantages of an enviable position to go and live among companions and under the authority of superiors whose birth and education are often quite inferior to one's own.[20]

17. Gertrude von Le Fort, *Song at the Scaffold*, trans. Emmet Lavery (New York: Samuel French, 1949).

18. Georges Bernanos, *The Heroic Face of Innocence*, trans. Pamela Morris and R. Batchelor (Grand Rapids, Mich.: William B. Eerdmans, 1999).

19. Ibid., p. 58.

20. Ibid.

Appendix D. Stage Manager's Handbook

A

Above
: A stage direction used in describing a position upstage (behind) furniture or scenery.

Aside
: Words spoken (or sung) not supposed to be heard by other members of the cast. Designated in the score in parentheses.

Assistant Stage Manager (A.S.M.)
: The A.S.M. is present at all rehearsals and during the run of a production helps make sure that all backstage activity runs smoothly, including actors' entrances as well as those of the chorus.

B

Batten
: Long horizontal pipes that hang above the stage from which curtains, lights, and flats are hung or secured.

Below
: A stage direction used to indicate a position downstage (in front) of furniture or scenery.

Blackout
: Lights are suddenly extinguished on the stage.

Black or Blacks
: Velvet curtains and borders used as a stage setting or for masking scenery.

Blocking
: The rough movements or "traffic patterns" of staging.

Book Flat
: Two flats hinged to fold like a book.

Border
: A length of painted canvas or other material such as velvet attached to a batten and suspended above the scene to conceal the top of the setting.

Business
: Actions performed by the actors in pantomime.

C

Call
: Indicates the time to arrive at the theater for costume and/or makeup. Can also indicate rehearsal ready time.

Center Line
: A line from the center of the playing stage area to the back wall.

Character Part
: A distinctive role (age, class) of a secondary nature.

Conception	A rehearsal common in German opera houses in which the director and designers explain their approach with renderings and models for the work about to be rehearsed.
Costume Parade	An event in varying forms of formality in which the costumes for a production are viewed under stage lights for the first time.
Costume Plot	A list of the characters and artists in the opera with details of costumes worn in each scene and act.
Counter	A stage direction indicating that the actor make an opposing movement (counter) to an actor who makes a cross.
Cover	The understudy "covers" the role played by another artist.
Cross-fade	A part of the scene darkens as another brightens.
Cue	The line of speech or action in the play that is a signal for another artist to begin speaking or an action to be performed.
Curtain Line	The line across the stage where the curtain meets the stage floor.
Cyc	Short for cyclorama: a neutral curtain placed at the back of the stage to give the impression of depth. With the properties of a screen, it can be lit to create atmosphere.

D

Dark	A theater that does not have a performance on a particular night is said to be "dark."
Door Flat	A flat containing a space for a door unit. (It is important to know which way the door opens before rehearsal begins.)
Dresser	A person assigned to help the actor properly put on and use the costume in the dressing room.
Dressing	Stage decoration or props *not* used in the action of the play.
Drop	Usually painted muslin hung at the back of the stage to create atmosphere.

F

False Proscenium	A semipermanent structure of two wings and a framed border set upstage of the theater proscenium.
Flat	The unit piece of scenery made of painted canvas on a wooden frame.
Flies	The space above the stage, including one or two galleries from which hanging scenery is lowered to or raised from the stage.

Fly Gallery	The narrow platform high above the stage floor running from the proscenium to the back wall. The space is used for hauling the ropes in flying scenery. Also called the fly door.
Follow Spots	Instruments that are hand-operated from the back of the house focused on one actor at a time. The spot is adjustable, and color (gels) are usually added.
Footlights	The rows of lamps with reflectors and frames for mediums enclosed in a metal trough along the front edge of the stage.
Fourth Wall	The imaginary wall in the opening of the proscenium arch.

G

Gel	A plastic filter used to give color to light shining through it. Colors are usually divided into cool light (blue tints) and warm light (amber tints) to show time of day and/or mood.
Gobo	A disklike device inserted into a lighting instrument to create various patterns in the light that is cast.
Going Up!	The stage manager's call warning the company that the curtain will rise in thirty minutes.

H

Hand Props	Properties carried by the artists.

I

Iris Down	The follow spot shrinking down smaller.
Iron Curtain	The fireproof safety curtain. It is the most downstage curtain.

L

Leg	The fabric hanging piece used to mask or hide the wings from the sight of the audience.
Lightwalker	Person who walks through staging when lighting levels are set by the lighting designer and director and cues are set by the stage manager.

M

Maestro	Generally used to refer to the conductor of the orchestra.
Main	The main curtain usually travels horizontally, vertically (guillotine), or "swagged" by pulleys.
Mask	To hide from view.

N

Notes   Generally given by the stage director after the rehearsal
                       to give the singer feedback concerning the performance
                       and adjustment suggestions before the next rehearsal.
                       The conductor might participate in the notes session.

O

Off Book   Memorized.
Offstage   Can refer to the wings or away from the center of the
                       stage.
Onstage   Can refer to an entrance onto the stage or toward the
                       center of the stage.

P

Personal Props   Hand properties that are provided by the management
                       but are looked after by the artists. Examples could be spec-
                       tacles, pocket watch, etc.
Practical   A fireplace that has an electric light to simulate a flame
                       or a window that opens is said to be practical.
Preset   Furniture and properties set on the stage in the scene be-
                       fore the curtain rises are said to be preset.
Producer   The person who puts everything together, from the
                       financial and business side to the scheduling and prepa-
                       ration of the musical/dramatic and technical produc-
                       tion. The responsibility for the whole production lies
                       with the producer.
Prologue   Introduction of the play or opera.
Prompt   To help an actor by throwing out key opening words or
                       phrases to stimulate the actor's memory. The actor will
                       intone the word "line" when memory fails.
Properties   Objects outside of the set and costumes used to further
                       the drama.
Proscenium   The opening of the stage through which the audience
                       views the play.

Q

Quick Change   A booth or station in the wings for an actor to make a
                       quick costume change. Helping is a "dresser."

R

Rake   The slope of the stage running downwards from the back
                       wall to the front of the stage. The rake is measured in de-
                       grees.

Read-through	An assembly of the entire cast to read and/or sing through the entire piece on book/score.
Restore	After a scene ending with a fadeout or blackout, for the lights to go on again for a curtain call.
Revolve	A revolving circular stage.
Run	The number of times or weeks a piece is presented; the length of time from the opening curtain to the closing curtain.
Run-through	A rehearsal in which the intent of the director or conductor is to go from the beginning to end without pause.

S

Scene	The act is broken down into scenes. The delineation of scenes is determined by change of place and/or time, and sometimes by the entrance and exit of characters.
Scrim	Gauzelike fabric with many uses. It is hung and "flown in" and has properties to be either transparent or opaque depending upon how it is lit.
Sight Line	The view of the actors, the stage, the set, and furniture from different places in the auditorium, especially far left, right, and balcony views.
Sitzprobe	A rehearsal with orchestra in which the singers concentrate on working with the conductor and orchestra without dramatic action.
Stage Cloth	A large sheet of canvas covering the stage area. It is also called a ground cloth.
Stage Manager (S.M.)	Present from the beginning to notate all stage actions of the actors and chorus. The S.M. is responsible for the smooth running of all rehearsals and performances. The S.M. also notates lighting cues and often "calls the show" from the stage manager's booth offstage. The S.M. calls actors to places, maintains order and quiet backstage, and is responsible for all called cues, including curtains and auditorium light cues. The S.M. is often assisted by an Assistant Stage Manager (A.S.M.).
Staging	A term that is used to connote a rehearsal beyond blocking, or "traffic patterns." Staging implies characterization and intent, relationships, and dramatic analyzation.
Strike	To take down and put away the sets and costumes after they have been used. Also, to remove from the stage any property or furniture when it is no longer needed.

Supers	The supernumeraries engaged for a scene who usually are involved in stage "business" and do not speak lines. Often they are recruited by the S.M.

T

Teaser	A strip of cloth to hide lighting instruments and hung scenery.
Technical Director (T.D.)	The person responsible for the scenic elements of the production, including the assembly of the set and the co-ordination of all scenic changes. Usually his or her responsibilities include the supervision of stage hands to execute the assembly and changes.
Tech Rehearsal	A stage rehearsal at the beginning of the rehearsals in the house. This rehearsal is most often with piano and emphasizes the technical elements of the production, coordinating lighting and sets with called cues. This rehearsal can be in costume.
Thrust Stage	A stage that projects into the audience area of the theater.
Traps	The trapdoors in the floor of the stage.

W

Walk-through	To rehearse a scene to go through movement coordination for mechanics and memory.
Wandelprobe	Same as *Sitzprobe,* but the performers work through a rough blocking of their actions. This is usually arranged by locating the orchestra in the pit and the singers onstage.
Wardrobe Mistress	Person in charge of the wardrobe and dressers and responsible for maintenance of the costumes.
Wings	The stage space offstage right and left and out of the sight of the audience.

Appendix E. Stage Combat:
Faints, Falls, and Fights

Dale Girard is a well-known combat director and choreographer as well as educator. He has staged fight scenes in the operas *Faust, Roméo et Juliette, Carmen, Macbeth, Don Giovanni,* and *Lucia di Lammermoor,* and in many plays. As an educator, he is an advocate for working on effective and safe stagecraft, and in staging hand-to-hand combat, knife, rapier, and dagger techniques as well as faints, falls, and stage violence. He has taught at Yale University, the Hartt School, the North Carolina School of the Arts, the University of Colorado, University of Denver, Harvard University, and the Banff Center. Mr. Girard's workshops have been repeated regularly each summer in the training centers of Central City Opera and Chautauqua Opera. The following exercises come from his workshops.

Warm-ups

E.1 FREE ARM TWIST

Objective: Releasing the knees, the spine, and the shoulder girdle.

Directions: Standing with legs apart, release the knees, and let the arms go. Twist the torso from the hips back and forth, letting the arms go in a free swing back and forth. Release the shoulders, breathe, and release the groin. The power comes from the floor.

E.2 WHIRLYBIRD

Objective: Freeing the shoulder/arm tension.

Directions: Similar to the free arm twist stance, rotate the arms over the head like a bicycle wheel going one way and then reverse, like the backstroke in swimming.

E.3 KNEE ROTATION

Objective: Feeling flexibility in the feet and ankles, and working the muscles of the thighs without putting weight on the knee joints.

Directions: Stand with feet together. The hands are placed right above the knee. Bend the knees slightly and rotate the hips and knees together with the feet stationary. Work the hips and quadriceps without putting pressure on the knees.

E.4 LUNGE AND BALANCE

Objective: Working the musculature needed for these routines, especially the quadriceps muscles, and the required flexibility. Also to feel the important center of gravity of the body as it shifts.

Directions: Take a long step diagonally and bring the body in a stretch over the knee. Feel this stretch in the gluts and the quads. Let go of this in a sudden "listen to the floor" release.

Exercises

E.5 FALLING FORWARD TO THE KNEES

Objective: Falling while protecting the knees.

Directions: Bend the knees, and as the body begins a forward motion, keep the counterweight of the upper body leaning back slightly, in the manner of the old "limbo" game.

The balance center of weight should be distributed carefully and slowly at first. Use the feet and ankles for control. To complete the fall, continue the motion to the floor, allowing the feet and legs to slide quickly underneath you, while you "listen to the floor," with the torso and head. You do not want to go face to the floor (risking impact injury to the face), but sideways with the head turned to the floor. The sound of impact can be made with the musculature of the arms on the floor, not the bones of the hands.

E.6 FAINTING IN A CORKSCREW FALL

Objective: Fainting without harm.

Directions: From the standing position the faint begins with the body twisting slightly in one direction or the other in a down position over one of the knees. The body then shifts its weight slightly to the other side of the body, while the leg the body is over initially releases forward and the toes are released. The body then basically can roll from a seated position back to the floor. It is best if this slow roll occurs on one side of the body or the other—not straight back on the spine, because opera costumes usually have a large zipper for many dresses and gowns at the center of the back, and this could cause injuries.

The faint is thus a smooth motion to the floor with realistic "stops" on the way down to the floor. Make sure you let go of the abdominal muscles and melt into the floor. Once again, the impact sound can come from the musculature of the arms striking the floor alongside the body (not the hands). Timing is very important.

E.7 SIT DOWN BACK FALL

Objective: Falling back by using the body counterweight. The fall is controlled and becomes less dangerous.

Directions: If you are not wearing a tight-fitting gown or dress around the knees, bring one leg back to expand your base, sit into the inner thigh, shift your weight to the other side, and roll down the side of the body (shifted weight side) while using the arms to reach forward as a counterweight toward the extended leg. After the body rolls down, the arms can make the sound of impact on the floor. Remember, the buttocks go down first, then the arms forward. The inclination will be for the arms to brace for impact, but this will bring your center of gravity back too fast. Remember to breathe out during this. Do not hold the breath. If you are wearing a tight-fitting dress, squat directly down over the bent knee so you are almost hugging it before rolling down on the other side.

E.8 FLYING SEAT DROP

Objective: Slipping on something, a comical fall without harm.

Directions: One leg upon "slipping" flies up; then sit back with your body as a counterweight and reach toward the extended leg, sitting back into the posted leg while lowering the body to the floor; arms make the impact sound while rolling back (again, be careful of the costume's zipper).

E.9 FALLING ON FACE

Objective: Presenting the illusion of falling after tripping. If gravity is involved, it is wrong.

Directions: After tripping, one leg goes forward to "catch" the body as you continue a lunge forward; "break" at waist, shift weight, and "listen to the floor." On going down to the floor, turn the head toward the extended leg side.

E.10 SHOVE FROM BEHIND

Objective: Engaging in two-actor stage business that has the illusion of violent energy but is controlled and safe.

Directions: The actor is approached from behind. In practicing this, make sure that you "check in" with the person you are about to shove down. Does this person have back problems or a shoulder injury, etc., that you should know about? The steps are as follows:

1. Stepping behind, make a strong "grab" of the triceps on both sides.
2. The head goes to the side, avoiding an accidental head butt by the person you are grabbing.
3. The elbows of the person behind go out and up (chicken wings) to show an illusion of gathering energy and intent.
4. The hands slide down the arms from the triceps with intensity as the person in front performs the first fall to the knees.

E.11 SHOVE BACKWARDS

Objective: Pushing the actor backwards to a sit down back fall without harm.

Directions: The actor once again approaches another actor, this time face to face. Again, make sure that the face of the one who pushes is to one side of the other actor to avoid accidental contact. Once again, "chicken wing" the arms before pushing to build the illusion of a dramatic "pickup" of momentum, and then bring your arms in a downward/outward motion as the other actor performs the backwards sit down fall. It is important for the person who shoves to feel grounded. Although there is no real force felt, this should look like there is a line of energy to the backwards fall.

E.12 SLAPPING THE ACTOR WITH A HAND/GLOVE

Objective: Slapping without harm.

Directions: When the actor slaps another actor with a glove (as in *La Traviata*), the glove should strike the downstage shoulder, only without swinging toward the head. If the actor simply strikes the shoulder, at the same time the person being struck should simply turn the head upstage at the sound of impact.

An actor should never slap another actor onstage. It is too dangerous. Again, rather than a swing (which will be only an illusion), the arm will extend straight out to the side of the face of the person you are slapping. As Girard says, "Air does not bleed." The person being slapped executes the "nap," or sound of the slap, by a quick clap of the hands. The head turns at "impact" during the nap.

Bibliography

Balk, H. Wesley. *The Complete Singer-Actor.* 2d ed. Minneapolis: University of Minnesota Press, 1985.

————. *Performing Power.* Minneapolis: University of Minnesota Press, 1985.

Beaumarchais, Pierre-Augustin Caron de. *Le Barbier de Seville* and *Le Marriage de Figaro.* Translated by Graham Anderson. Bath: Absolute Press, 1993.

Belasco, David. *Madame Butterfly.* Boston: Little, Brown, 1928.

Bernanos, Georges. *The Heroic Face of Innocence.* Translated by Pamela Morris and R. Batchelor. Grand Rapids, Mich.: William B. Eerdmans, 1999.

Brian, Experience. "Stanislavsky and the Classical Singer." *Classical Singer*, October 2000.

The Carmelite Martyrs of Compiègne. Dublin: Carmelite Publications, n.d.

Chekhov, Michael. *On the Technique of Acting.* Edited by Mel Gordon. New York: HarperCollins, 1991.

Chisman, Isabel, and Hester E. Raven-Hart. *Manners and Movements in Costume Plays.* Boston: Walter H. Baker, 2000.

Cole, Toby, ed. *Actors on Acting.* New York: Crown, 1954.

Dornemann, Joan, with Maria Ciaccia. *Complete Preparation: A Guide to Auditioning for Opera.* New York: Excalibur, 1992.

Dumas *fils*, Alexandre. *Camille, the Lady of the Camellias.* Translated by Edmond Gosse. New York: Signet Classics, 1984.

Kohlhaas, Karen. *The Monologue Audition: A Practical Guide for Actors.* New York: Limelight, 2000.

MacDonald, Glynn. *Alexander Technique.* Dorset: Element Books, 1998.

Mérimée, Prosper. *Carmen and Other Stories.* Translated by Nicholas Jotcham. New York: Oxford University Press, 1989.

Milcheel, Theresa. *Movement: From Person to Actor to Character.* Lanham, Md.: Scarecrow Press, 1995.

Morris, Desmond. *Gestures.* New York: Stein and Day, 1979.

Mürger, Henri. *Scènes de la vie de bohème.* Translated by Elizabeth Ward Hugus. Westport, Conn.: Hyperion Press, 1978.

The Music Theater of Walter Felsenstein. Translated by Peter Paul Fuchs. New York: W. W. Norton, 1975.

Payne, Blanche. *The History of Costume.* New York: HarperCollins, 1992.

Penrod, James. *Movement for the Performing Artist.* Palo Alto, Calif.: National Press Books, 1974.

Pierce, Alexandra, and Roger Pierce. *Generous Movement.* Redlands, Calif.: Center of Balance Press, 1991.

Poggi, Jack. *The Monologue Workshop.* New York: Applause Books, 1990.

Rubin, Lucille S., ed. *Movement for the Actor.* New York: Drama Book Specialists, 1980.

Russell, Douglas A. *Period Style for the Theatre.* Boston: Allyn and Bacon, 1980.

Sardou, Victorien. *La Tosca.* Translated by W. Laird Kleine-Ahlbrandt. New York: Edwin Mellen Press, 1990.

Shakespeare, William. *Henry IV, Part One.* Edited by David Bevington. New York: Bantam Books, 1988.

Silverberg, Larry. *The Sanford Meisner Approach.* Hanover, N.H.: Smith and Kraus, 2000.

Smith, Marias, and Kristin Graham, eds. *Monologues from Literature: A Sourcebook for Actors.* New York: Ballantine Books, 1990.

Spolin, Viola. *Improvisation for the Theater.* 3d ed. Evanston, Ill.: Northwestern University Press, 1999.

Suzuki, Tadashi. *The Way of Acting.* Translated by J. Thomas Rimer. New York: Theatre Communications Group, 1986.

Van Witsen, Leo. *Costuming for Opera.* Bloomington: Indiana University Press, 1981.

Von Le Fort, Gertrude. *Song at the Scaffold.* Adapted for the stage by Emmet Lavery. New York: Samuel French, 1949.

White, Edwin C., and Marguerite Battye. *Acting and Stage Movement.* Colorado Springs, Colo.: Meriwether, 1985.

Yordon, Judy. *Roles in Interpretation.* Boston: McGraw-Hill, 2002.

Index

Page numbers in italic type denote exercises.

A teacher and director, Mark Ross Clark has taught opera workshop for twenty years and has directed and produced more than fifty operas in professional and university venues. He holds a doctorate in opera production and degrees in vocal performance and vocal pedagogy; he is currently Associate Professor in the Indiana University School of Music. He has held singer-getic workshops at universities and young artist programs throughout the United States.